the overlook martial arts handbook

the overlook martial arts handbook

David Mitchell

THE OVERLOOK PRESS
Woodstock, New York

Dedication

This book is dedicated to the memory of the late Jim Elkin who was not only a leading martial artist but was one of the still rarer minority who generously give of their time and effort to help make the practice of the martial arts more enjoyable and meaningful for the majority.

First published in 1988 by
The Overlook Press
Lewis Hollow Road
Woodstock, New York 12498

Library of Congress Cataloging-in-Publication Data

Mitchell, David 1944–
The Overlook martial arts handbook

Reprint. Originally published: The official martial
arts handbook, 1984.
Includes index.
1. Martial arts. I. Mitchell, David, 1944–
Official martial arts handbook. II. Title. III. Title:
Martial arts handbook.
GV1102.M58 1988 796.8 87-11087
ISBN 0-87951-285-7

CONTENTS

INTRODUCTION

The term 'martial arts' means those arts concerned with the waging of war; yet curiously, very few listed in these pages meet that definition. By far the majority are relatively recent activities, developed in the twentieth century itself and having only the smallest connection with the battlefield.

Some of the recorded activities were martial arts in the days of the bow and arrow but through the passage of time, the purpose in practising them has altered. Although they no longer had a military role, it was said that their study would develop character, or higher moral standards. As a result of this change they ceased to have any military connotation and became a martial art 'way' instead.

The Japanese activity known as Kendo was once a martial art. It was originally practised as Kenjitsu, which taught the warrior armed with a sword how to survive on the field of battle. Kendo itself however, is not a martial art, Kyu Jitsu, or archery technique was the means by which the Japanese warrior killed his enemies with a bow and arrow. The activity, known as Kyudo which derives from it is no longer concerned about where the arrows fly so long as the posture and form are correct. Those who study Kyudo confirm that it is not a martial art.

The unarmed Japanese 'compliant techniques' of Jiu Jitsu played only a very minor role on the battlefield, offering at best the means of capturing a warrior alive. They were not sophisticated and found their best application in the hands of merchants. The best known school of Jiu Jitsu, Judo, lost very little time in denying any link with the martial arts, preferring to be known as a 'Combat Sport'. Shorinji Kempo is deeply concerned with the religion devised by its founder. It has never been used on a battlefield.

Karate is one of the most popular activities coming from the Far East. It was originated to deal with thieves and local villains. Shortly after being introduced to mainland Japan, it was changed a great deal and became a martial art way. Karate's only connection with the battlefield came through it being taught to conscripts, with the intention of increasing their martial ardour!

In Korea, the years of Japanese occupation seem to have suppressed and replaced the native arts with systems similar to Karate and Aikido. In 1955, a new combat system was originated and saw limited use in the Korean War. This system

Gichin Funakoshi, the founder of Karatedo

was called Taekwondo and a rigorous military programme of training ensured that every soldier received a basic knowledge.

The Chinese martial arts were once used on the battlefield and were clearly demonstrated in the great deeds of the Shaolin warrior monks. Many of these ancient techniques are preserved today in much the same way as they were practised then. They have little underlying philosophy – just a desire to prove effective against the opponent. Of course they are no longer of any use on a modern battlefield but neither have they been softened or changed through the introduction of quasi-religious principles.

In the light of this, the title martial art seems inappropriate; but what is the alternative? As in the case of the nonsense term 'Kung Fu' which has become widely accepted to describe the Chinese martial arts, so has the term 'martial art' come to mean that which it largely is not.

The Japanese warrior in his lacquered bamboo armour

Regardless of the terms used, the practice of the 'martial arts' has mushroomed in recent years. There are many reasons for this. Television and films showing one man's incredible feats of oriental fighting have captured the imagination of thousands of impressionable youngsters and hinted that there are mysterious alternatives to the well known boxing and wrestling; alternatives that will apparently allow them to smash through bricks and deal with uncountable attackers with the slightest effort.

Women, more realistically, were drawn to the martial arts as a means of protecting themselves from violence without becoming part of it. The restrictions on female martial artists have been crumbling since the early 1970s although they have by no means disappeared.

In the majority of cases, people taking up a martial art

activity do so in ignorance of the principles upon which the system is built. Once in membership, the well defined structure, the atmosphere and the gradual steps towards the coveted black belt capture the imagination. Few students ever come to realise the full potential of what they are learning. Furthermore, because the concepts underlying some martial art activities are foreign, few take them up. After all, it is difficult enough to fill a traditional church, without expecting average people to embrace the ideas of Zen, or the Tao. As a result, what happens is that people learn the techniques but don't learn the art. They are like the student of Tai Chi Chuan who trains for thirty years and masters all the movements, yet never succeeds in controlling the Chi. Such technicians, no matter how good, will never approach the skills of the founders.

Sporting activities have come to take the place of many deeper concepts. The martial art activity may well have turned towards competition and in consequence, has attracted a greater following of students keen to win medals and play at fighting. Self defence activities are also popular but without the deeper concepts, these too are incomplete.

In order to learn the martial arts, the student must look deeper than the mere copying of physical techniques.

JAPAN

1. THE WEAPON ARTS

Budo

A study of Japan's history shows it to be a country which, for long periods of time, was totally obsessed with fighting. Battles were fought between rival groups of warriors, the noblest caste of ancient Japan. Not only were there warriors, there were also the peasants, the merchants and the 'unspeakables'. Of all these, the warrior Bushi were the noblest and from their ranks came Japan's military rulers. Even within the warrior caste there were ranks, with the Samurai originally being one such. Later on, the word 'Samurai' came to be used to describe any true warrior.

The best were able to trace their family lineage back many generations, whilst the not so good were soon eliminated during the periods of deadly fighting. To maintain their pre-eminent rank, the Bushi families needed more than political sense and good breeding; they needed to be properly skilled in the techniques of war — otherwise known as 'Bujitsu'. Skilled warriors were in great demand to teach the young of the noble houses the skills of Bujitsu, namely horseriding, archery and swordsmanship.

Having been born into the warrior caste, the Bushi were expected to be able to perform all, not just some of the techniques of Bujitsu. Each warrior balanced on his horse whilst carrying a bow and arrow and in addition, three or more swords and a host of daggers! The bow was used from a distance and the swords for closer work. An especially long sword allowed the rider to cut down dismounted warriors, whilst a short sword allowed the warrior to remain effectively armed whilst indoors.

Even the women of the noble house were expected to fight if the need arose and so they were taught the use of the spear, the naginata (a kind of spear with a cutting edge), the sword and the knife. Disarmed warriors were captured using a form of unarmed combat taught as part of their training. The system took into account the fact that armour was worn and so grappling, rather than striking techniques were required.

e Kendo fighter in armour

The warriors who taught Bujitsu knew that their techniques worked on the battlefield, for that is where they themselves had achieved success. Large numbers of ideas and strategies were combined into a particular teaching syllabus, or Ryu, aimed at making the warrior into an unbeatable fighter. It was only after the setting up of the Tokugawa Shogunate in the early 17th century that the martial arts went into a decline.

The Shogun was the military ruler of Japan and whilst he paid homage to the Emperor, this was merely a courtesy. The first Tokugawa Shogun, Ieyasu, proved to be a cunning ruler. He saw the danger of having large numbers of skilled warrior armies, each under the control of the local lords (some of whom were not supporters of the Shogunate). Therefore, by means of careful alliances, he bought time enough to reduce the importance and stature of the Bushi.

The size of a lord's personal army was thereafter limited and members of his family were obliged to spend periods at the Shogun's court – ostensibly as guests but actually as hostages. The lords themselves were compelled to spend a period of the year at the court and found the financial burden thus levied, to be as heavy as the Shogun had intended it to be.

With the suppression of wars, the warriors became less used and eventually, through stagnation, less proficient. Even the fighting of duels came to be frowned upon and the erstwhile warriors of the battlefield were encouraged to become warriors of the poem. To the warrior, the sword was the embodiment of spirit and valour and when a force of highly trained Bushi armed with swords was cut down by a conscript army of peasants armed with guns, it became obvious that the old military ways were no longer applicable.

The Bushi therefore turned to 'martial art ways', or Budo, in place of their beloved Bujitsu. The warrior, deprived of his right to triumph with sword on the battlefield became the warrior of the dojo, or 'place of training in the Way'. The only possibility of combat arose through a combat sport. In place of the live blade, where a mistake meant death or hideous injury, bamboo swords and protective armour allowed a warrior to be safely killed several times in the course of a training session. Kenjitsu, the technique of sword-fighting became Kendo, the Way of the Sword.

It was no longer required to triumph over the enemy – it became more important to triumph over oneself. Thus the martial art ways were used to develop selflessness; an unawareness of self that led to instinctive and effective action.

It was said that a student could learn all the techniques and be no more than a good technician. The important thing was to go beyond the stage of mastering mere techniques and to train the mind and body so well that one entered a new state of consciousness. Readers familiar with Eastern philosophy will readily recognise the influence of Zen here.

In changing over from the 'Jitsu' to the 'Do', the study of the martial arts became less concerned with the necessities of life and death and more concerned with the mental and spiritual development of the student.

Kobudo

The term 'Kobudo' means simply, 'Old Martial Art Ways.' It is used to describe the study of classical Japanese and Okinawan weaponry. Some of the weaponry was covert; that is to say, it was designed to be mistaken by the authorities for simple tools. Other types were quite obviously weapons but were not used widely by the warriors.

Many of the covert weapons were developed in Okinawa, when the latter was subjugated by Japan. As a means of self protection, the islanders took up Okinawa Hand. This art included the use of various covert weapons, such as an oaken staff. This six-foot length of smooth, dense wood was used to balance heavy loads on the shoulders so it is thicker in the middle for more comfortable carrying and tapered toward the ends for lightness and ease of handling.

The staff was primarily an outdoor weapon requiring a fair amount of space to employ it with any reasonable degree of success. In use, it formed an extension to the empty hand moves of the body, lending them extra length and rigidity. The staff was powered by the body movement of the holder, rather than relying upon the weight and momentum of the weapon. Several of the moves seen in Karate katas show the hands grasping at an imaginary staff and using it in this manner.

The Japanese staff was made of highly polished Japanese oak. It was swung viciously through the air and could quite easily shatter a sword blade, or break bones. The classical Japanese warrior found the six foot staff valuable in teaching the concept of effective distance. Used against a swordsman, it was effective as long as the blade was kept at a distance. It could even be used to attack an armoured warrior, using strong thrusts of the butt to drive between the armour plates. A

The Japanese staff. Use is made of its weight and it is swung in vicious arcs

variation of the Japanese staff was the iron staff. This weighty weapon was used to develop strength in the arms and upper body. Its weight made it suitable for use by only the strongest of warriors. It was particularly effective at dispersing a group of opponents when swung in wide arcs.

Not found in Okinawa was the shorter stick, or Jo. This is described in the section dealing with Aikido, where it is used both as a weapon and as a means to develop wrist flexibility. The jo is about four feet in length and when two are skilfully deployed, the user can handle just about any other classical weapon exponent. Because the jo is light, it can be whirled extremely quickly, blocking and striking in quick succession.

The Sai is a characteristic weapon of Okinawa-Te. It is a three pronged fork, with the central tine much longer than the two laterals. The handle is weighted and makes quite a good truncheon, whilst the tines are sharp and penetrate flesh easily. A sword blade, caught between them, may be broken by means of a twisting action. The sai are used in pairs and are tailor-made for the individual. The central tine lies along the forearm, where it can deflect a strike by the staff. The sai can also be thrown short distances and it is said that criminals

The Sai are used in pairs and can be used both to block and to pierce

caught in the act had their feet literally nailed to the ground by it.

Because of its characteristics, this weapon proved ideal to Okinawa-Te practitioners. Some schools practised a quick draw method of pulling the sai from the belt, using and returning it in one smooth movement. The classical karateka used them in kata, snapping them forward to strike with the point, or swivelling them back and using the clubbed end. They can also be used in an 'X' block, where they cross over above the head, or in front of the groin.

A variation of the sai has one of the lateral tines reversed. This variant is known as the 'Manji-no-Sai'. Occasionally the weapon is mounted on the end of a pole, making a composite capable of ensnaring the clothes of a fugitive. The origin of the sai has been traced back to Indonesia and China from where it was probably introduced to Okinawa by sailors.

The sickle is used as a weapon in both Okinawan and Japanese Kobudo. In Okinawa, the farmer normally carried them in pairs. It has a long hardwood handle, with a short blade at one end. The blade projects at right angles to the

The Tonfa are swung by means of the pegs which are located towards their lower ends

handle and may be slightly curved. Only the inner edge is a cutting edge. Uses of the sickle include a piercing, a cutting or a clubbing action. Unusually, the sickle can be held parallel to the forearm with the blade jutting outwards for close work. The Japanese sickle was used singly and had a long weighted chain hanging from the haft. The chain was used to ensnare the opponent so that the sickle part could then be used. The weapon was difficult to use and formed part of an armoury of speciality weapons.

The rice grinder handles, or 'Tonfa' are described in the chapter dealing with Jiu Jitsu. These weapons are peculiar to Okinawa-Te but it is by no means unusual to see them now being used by other systems. They are ideal for Karate practice, being primarily close quarter weapons which strengthen the block and strike.

The fan is an unlikely weapon but it was occasionally used as such by the Japanese warrior. Sometimes the warrior had to leave his swords outside in order to enter a dwelling. When this happened, he would take a fan with him. The fan, or 'Tessen' as it was called, was made of iron and sometimes designed so that it could be opened out. It was used rather like a short stick and could be used to ward off a knife attack.

The Rice Flails are whirled around in a confusing pattern of movement which covers all possible targets

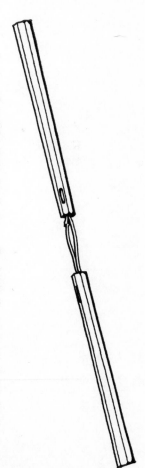

Perhaps the best known of all covert weapons is the rice flail, or 'Nun-Chaku'. This implement, used ostensibly to thresh rice, consists of two hardwood batons (which may be round or octagonal in section). The original nun-chaku used a simple hinge to join the two batons, so that it could only snap open or closed, but under Chinese influence the flexible thong was introduced. This allowed the weapon to be used in a more effective way for keeping would-be attackers at a manageable distance.

The batons can both be grasped in one hand and used like a single stick to club or jab. Alternatively, one baton can be released, to be swung in a bewildering series of figure-eights in front and behind the user. A great deal of practice is necessary to transfer the baton from one hand to another, without interrupting the smooth flow of movement. The linkage of the nun-chaku can be used to entrap another weapon and it may also be used as a garrotte.

Two rather similar types of weapon are the Okinawan Tekki and the Japanese Tekkan-Zu. The tekki are spiked metal knuckledusters whilst the tekkan-zu are metal rings, used by some Taijitsu schools for delivering atemi strikes.

Spears were found in both Japanese and Okinawan martial

art systems. In Okinawa, the spear was a short, stabbing instrument, often used in conjunction with a round shield. In Japan, the spear was a much longer weapon, used primarily by the lower caste warriors. The original spears proved unsuitable and so later designs located the point deeply in the haft, where it was secured with binding. Some spears were made with hooks below the tip. These were used to catch, or cut the opponent.

A similar weapon to the spear was the Naginata. This consisted of a long shaft, at the end of which was a single-edged, curved blade. An earlier version of the naginata used a shorter shaft. Both were used extensively by the warriors and in particular by the lower caste soldiers. They were useful against the mounted rider but had the disadvantage of being heavy annd unwieldy. Both the spear and the naginata were useful weapons for dealing with someone at a distance but once that distance was closed, they were less effective than the sword. In later years, the naginata was relegated to home defence and women were taught its use.

Kendo

Kendo means 'The Way of the Sword'. It is derived from a previous martial art and in this case, the martial art was 'Kenjitsu'. To appreciate the significance of Kendo in Japan, it is necessary to look at its history.

The sword was said to represent the soul of the warrior. It was the weapon of choice, used during hand to hand combat with the opponent. The warrior was allowed to wear two swords, the longer for normal use and the shorter for use in enclosed spaces.

Originally, the Japanese sword was straight, the characteristic curvature being introduced somewhere around the tenth century. The two thwarted Mongol invasions of Japan not only caused a temporary unification of the warring clans, they also led to a development in the warrior's sword. The pre-invasion swords incorporated the stabbing tip with the blade edge, so that if the tip was broken off, as frequently happened on the Mongol armour, the sword was rendered useless. Later designs sharpened the tip separately from the blade and this left the sword effective even once the tip had been broken off.

During the late sixteenth century, Korean metal workers were brought to Japan. These skilled workers used the principle of compression forging, the result of which was to produce a much harder and denser steel. The way in which this was achieved was by hammering out the ingot and then cutting it virtually in half along its length. The halves were then folded, so as to lie together and hammered flat again. The process was repeated many times before the final shape of the blade was formed. The sword was then embossed on the haft with a design identifying the swordsmith. Swords designed for rich families sometimes also had a beautiful design cut into the blade with a chisel. After forging, the blades were sent for polishing and to be fitted with a finger guard, or 'Tsuba' and a handle.

The Kendoka on the right cuts cleanly to 'Men'

The warriors using these swords came from a distinct caste, which included the 'Bushi', or warriors of noble birth. These were assisted by lower grade warriors, such as the 'Samurai', or assistants to the nobility. In recent times, the role of the Samurai has been elevated. At the time when warriors were becoming scarce – as in the Age of Wars – it was not uncommon to press gang members of the lower castes into becoming low grade warriors. These unfortunates were armed as cheaply as possible and were normally issued spears, rather than the beloved sword.

There were literally hundreds of different swordfighting schools, all concerned with their own special techniques. Some favoured cutting at the legs and groin, others attacked the wrists and hands. The more successful schools concentrated upon continuous aggression, subjecting the opponent to a concentrated attack which led to him making mistakes.

The less effective but more popular schools favoured a cautious, 'wait and see' attitude. Regardless of the school, there was a need to practise the various techniques and so formalised patterns, or Kata, were made up. These were supplemented by using the oaken sword, or Bokken.

To reduce the incidence of injury whilst practising with a partner, an attempt was made to create a lighter sword, using bamboo strips covered with animal skin. Heavy gauntlets were used to protect the wrists and eventually a padded helmet appeared. These were refined in the 18th century by Chuzo Nakanishi, into the Kendo armour that is used today. Kendo armour consists of a lacquered 'Do' or breastplate, a pair of gauntlets which are known as 'Kote' and a helmet with a steel grid protecting the face. The latter is known as 'Men'.

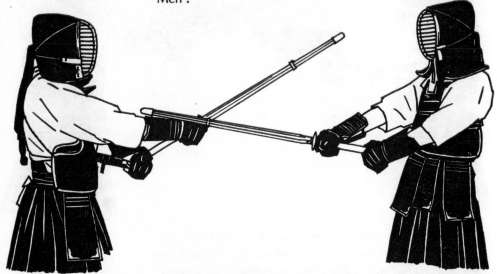

A cut to the wrist ('Kote')

The modern bamboo sword, or Shinai, consists of bamboo strips united at the tip, with a guard and grip at the other end. These weapons are approximately 45"–46" in length and are very light. This lightness allows them to be moved extremely quickly – far more quickly than the longsword. They also differ from the longsword in that they have no curvature and are tubular in section. As a result of this, techniques with the shinai are quite different from those using the live blade.

The use of armour and a bamboo shinai meant that it was possible to engage in fierce combat, with little likelihood of injury. For this reason, the practice of fighting with shinais became immensely popular, replacing much of the older forms of study. As the Edo period progressed, commoners were encouraged to indulge in Kendo and did so with great enthusiasm. Several hundred dojos were set up for them.

Following this spread of interest, a great deal of competition took place between members of different schools. At first, competitions were haphazard in that the style of the armour and the length of the shinai had not yet been agreed. There were many competition-minded individuals who made a name (and some money for themselves) by going on a tournament-type circuit. Some even went from dojo to dojo, challenging the master to meet them in combat.

In this way, Kendo moved further and further away from the original idea which was improvement in swordsmanship, towards competition for competition's sake. The opportunities for actual sword fighting had diminished to practically zero and the carrying of swords began to appear more and more outdated. Frequently, swordsmen carrying their two swords were jeered at by rude commoners with the taunt that 'times have changed'. In the fifteenth and sixteenth centuries, such behaviour would have been unthinkable and the warrior expected to cut down those guilty of it. In the latter days of the Edo period, it became necessary to apply formally for permission to use the sword!

While the use of the sword decreased, that of the bamboo shinai increased, with would-be warriors encouraged to vent their warlike tendencies upon each other in the safety of the school. Eventually, rules defining the length of the shinai, the target areas to be attacked and the shape of the armour were introduced. A system of scoring was introduced and the door opened to proper competition. In spite of these advances, some older ryu maintained their own form of practice and insisted that the prime reason for studying Kendo was for the development of the practitioner's character.

A united Kendo governing body was set up in Japan. This set out a number of katas to be practised, taking them from original ryu. A great impetus for Kendo's development came through the Government's insistence on teaching it as a compulsory subject in Japanese schools and colleges as a way of strengthening the martial art spirit of the Japanese people prior to the Second World War. This same rationale was applied to naginata training for girls.

Kendo is now practised widely throughout the world and there are both continental and world championships.

Initial training in a Kendo dojo teaches the student how to stand correctly – with the right foot forward and the rear left foot resting with the heel very slightly raised. The purpose of this quite upright stance is to allow a sudden advance. A simple white Judo or Karate gi may be worn during the early lessons. Later, the student will add the hakama, a split skirt which is worn in conjunction with a gi jacket.

The Kendoka on the right cuts horizontally to 'Do'

Armed with a shinai, the student is encouraged to attack a senior grade repeatedly, the latter retreating passively. The purpose of this is to encourage aggression and to teach the correct distance and technique. Accompanying the blows, the student will shout 'Men!' if attacking the head, 'Do!' if attacking the breastplate and 'Kote!' if striking the gloves. The shout is important in focussing the student's aggression and contrary to other martial art ways, the shout, or 'Kiai' is high pitched and sounds like a shriek. This type of kiai is peculiar to the active Kendo dojo and allows the exact premises being used to be pinpointed by newcomers!

The form of the cut is important if a score is to be awarded.

A blow to men, for instance, must be followed through by passing the opponent and turning ready to attack again. Sometimes the opponent evidently does not agree that the cut was effective and strikes mightily at the attacker, as the latter passes with shinai held high.

In Kendo, the various ranks are not shown by coloured belts. The Kendo grade of first dan (first degree black belt) is not regarded as a senior qualification. The first dan has merely learned the very basic essentials needed to allow one to go on to develop through practice, the skill needed to reach the higher dan grades. It is not uncommon to find a large number of third and fourth dans in a typical, non-Japanese dojo.

Some Kendo practitioners are quite critical of certain habits developing in Kendo. They are for instance concerned over the habit of locking the elbows straight during a cut to men. This, it has been pointed out, would not result in a proper cut with a live blade. Instead, the shinai should be held relatively loosely and at the moment of the cut, the hands should clench tightly. An examination made during the practice of Suburi, or Cutting the Air illustrates the point of this criticism. Suburi is a basic part of Kendo practice and is often performed with the heavier oaken bokken. When done several hundred times, the action strengthens the wrists and arms.

Ji Geikon, or Free Practice takes up a great deal of time in the dojo. The armour necessary to take part is either loaned by the dojo, or more usually bought by the student. The armour is long lasting but the shinai tends to break after a while. Unbroken bits of the shinai should be kept and used to repair others.

Two kendoka begin their free practice together by bowing. They then approach each other and draw the shinai while assuming the squatting starting position sonkyo. A match is started from this position. The kendoka then stand and face each other in the ready position, with shinai held out and pointing to the opponent's throat or eye level.

From this position, attack may be launched using any one of the classic cuts, or the 'Tsuki' – a thrust with the straight shinai to the armoured throat of the opponent. In order to score, the cut should strike the scoring area directly and with good technique. A proper carry through must follow the successful cut. A cut will not score if it is diverted by the opponent's shinai, or if it is not made with correct form.

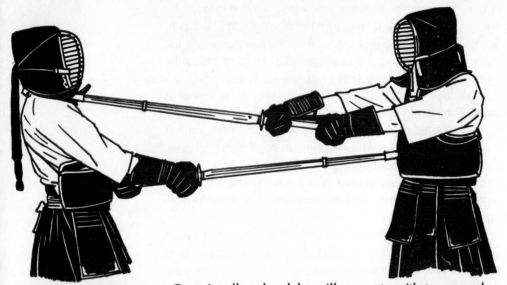

The Kendoka on the right performs 'Tsuki'. Note his extended arms

Occasionally a kendoka will compete with two swords. When this happens, the one sword is a normal shinai and the other, a much shorter bamboo blade. This form of combat is called Ni To and it requires great skill to perform properly. The tactics of Kendo competition are based upon a number of concepts. The first is waiting and attacking at the same time. This can be taken to mean the pressing home of a vigorous attack whilst looking for the inevitable openings offered by the opponent under pressure. Another is the open mind in attacking, which does not rely upon easily thwarted preconceived plans of what to do.

Awareness of the attacker will allow the good student to forestall an attack by engaging fiercely at the moment it was about to be launched. In order to do this, it is necessary to be able instinctively to identify the attacker's essential movements, rather than the diversionary feint. 'Kendo' it is said, 'is ferocious warfare; it is not merely an exercise'. In support of this claim it is common to see kendoka attacking with such strength that they crash into each other and thrusting strongly away, attempt to strike upon the disengagement (tai atari).

It is interesting to note that Kendo competition does not allow cutting to the legs. In mixed matches between shinai and the naginata however, shin pads are allowed, since the legs are a scoring target for the latter weapon. In the informal sparring of the dojo, furthermore, a brisk cut to the leg with the shinai from the instructor can do much to correct a bad stance.

Iaido

Iaido is a martial art way based upon the drawing of the long sword. It has arisen from the original techniques of Iai Jitsu, where the warrior was required to draw his sword quickly, strike down the opponent, shake off the blood from the blade and return it to its scabbard. It is in some ways similar to the gunfighter lore of the Wild West, where the quickest on the draw got in the first shot!

Being a martial art way, Iaido is not concerned with the effectiveness of the technique but rather it concentrates upon the development of perfect form, as laid down by the Japanese governing body. The sword is carried on the left side, in the belt, with the sharp edge uppermost. The practitioner kneels in the classic 'Seiza' position, with the feet extended out behind, the back upright. Before kneeling, the wings of the split skirt are swept out and the sheathed sword placed deferentially upon the floor. The practitioner bows before the sword, then picks it up in a prescribed manner and slides it into the belt.

After composing himself, the practitioner will smoothly unsheath the sword and cut an imaginary assailant. Following this, the blade is shaken to disperse the blood that would have collected on it; then it is smoothly and unfalteringly returned to the scabbard. This latter operation calls for very great practice, since the sword is guided into the scabbard by touch alone – the eyes do not deviate from looking towards the imaginary assailant. During this operation, the edge of the sword passes the tips of the fingers and the point must not catch the edge of the scabbard before it is slid home.

The actual cut may be made as a single movement, or the practitioner can turn about and cut a second time in a different direction before returning the blade. Whichever the case, the movement must appear natural, as though generated of itself.

It is very interesting to compare Iaido with its parent Iai Jitsu. The latter was not designed to operate from a position of seiza, since no warrior would have drawn his sword from a fully kneeling position. A quick move would have brought him up onto his one knee, with the sword available for instant use.

Usually in Iai Jitsu, the sword is drawn from the standing position with an extremely fast action. The cutting stroke must be truly effective and the way in which this is tested is against upright bamboo poles planted in the ground. Bags of straw are also used but during the days of the Bushi, the bodies of

The kneeling swordsman is attacked

executed criminals were used to practice on.

By turning abruptly with the hips, the practitioner of Iai Jitsu is able to test his ability to cut effectively in a variety of directions. Some of the ancient scrolls showing Iai Jitsu depict one man facing several. With the first draw, the sword is jabbed backwards into an opponent standing immediately behind. Despite the suddenness and accuracy of the strike, the defender's eyes remain looking towards the front as an overarm movement withdraws the blade and sends it obliquely through the second attacker's body at neck height. Without a pause, the blade continues through the midsection of the third attacker. At the conclusion of this, the defender would have slowly replaced the sword in its scabbard – much slower than the action of the modern Iaido man – whilst keeping his eyes fixed upon the fallen. The symbolic shaking off of the blood would have been replaced by a more thorough wiping of the blade with a piece of material.

Simultaneously rising and sidestepping, the defender draws his sword and cuts to the wrist

Kyudo

Kyudo is the martial art way of the bow. It is derived from the Kyu Jitsu of the Bushi, having originated when the bow was replaced by the musket. In Kyu Jitsu, the warrior considered accuracy to be the main achievement and practised using the bow whilst both mounted and dismounted. The curious shape of the Japanese bow is derived from the need for it to be used on horseback. The grip is closer to one end of the bow than the other so that it can be quickly transferred from one side of the horse to the other. Regardless of its asymmetric shape, the bow is made so as to provide an equal pull from both longer and shorter parts.

The modern Japanese bow comes in various lengths and is made up of laminated bamboo, its tension varying considerably according to requirement. The arrows are designed for use with the bow and are normally kept together in a lacquered wood, free-standing quiver. Each archer will take two arrows at a time and will discharge them with the aim of achieving perfect form. Accuracy is no longer the main issue. To achieve form, many hours are spent shooting arrows into the Makiwara — the latter being composed of bales of straw, or rolls of cardboard. These makiwara are only a few feet from the archer, allowing the retrieval of spent arrows without much effort.

The archer begins from the kneeling position, holding the bow well out from the body. With careful attention, the archer ensures that the arrow is correctly nocked and, holding it in place, rises to an upright position and surveys the target. The stance is carefully spaced out, with the feet sliding from side to side until the correct distance is achieved. The spare arrow is held back at the hip during this procedure, but in preparation for the draw it is held in the fingers.

To begin the draw, the bow is held high above the head and as it is lowered, both arms move apart so that the bow is drawn. As the arrow comes to lie alongside the side of the face, the string is released and the bow twists around in the

The kneeling archer in traditional attire

The bow at full draw

hand. The arm that drew the bow is extended backwards and this posture is held whilst the arrow flies to the target.

At all times, perfect posture must be in evidence. A total calmness must be apparent throughout and the release of the arrow must be a spontaneous act; it is not planned, it just happens. The archer must be careful not to let the arrow fall from its nocked position and there must be no quivering of the muscles if the bow is held at full draw for any length of time. It is not necessary to strike the bullseye, but a minimum standard of accuracy is required.

The atmosphere of the Kyudo training hall is one of quiet contemplation. Before the class begins to shoot in earnest, there is a period of kneeling meditation, followed by a salute to the target. To do this, groups of archers stand up and advance towards the target with lowered bow, feet skimming over the polished wood floor. They then kneel and at staggered intervals, nock the arrows, stand and discharge them at the distant target.

The uniform worn is always scrupulously clean, with typically white cotton tops worn above dark split skirts. In the case of the men, there is an open armpit to the jacket whilst the women wear a breast protector. A gauntlet is used in the drawing of the bow.

If a bowstring breaks during practice, a new one is fitted but this must be treated before it can be used. Additional layers of bowstring are carefully glued to the part the arrow's nock fits around to ensure a close fit.

Ninjitsu

The 'Ninja', or 'Stealers In' were the secret agents of ancient Japan. At first, the Ninja were a form of contract hire secret organisation, whose services could be bought by the highest bidder but when the advantages of such people were fully realised, the Bushi themselves set up training camps for their own, lower grade warriors.

The Ninja practised the techniques of 'Ninjitsu' which allowed them to scale sheer walls, drop from great heights without injury and kill by a variety of methods. The best Ninja were those who were trained from childhood; their pliable joints being manipulated so that they were capable of worming through gaps that the average person would have found impossible. Ninja weaponry included the knife, the short sword, the spear and a variety of throwing weapons such as the 'Shuriken', or 'Star Wheel'.

Ninja senses were trained to perfection, with keen eyesight and night vision aided by unusually acute hearing that could instantly detect a change in background noise – such as the sudden drop in the noise level of crickets in a particular area at night where otherwise noiseless infiltrators were at work. Even the manner in which they moved was rigorously conditioned so that they could cross sprung wooden floors silently and without squeaks.

When caught, the Ninja could expect no mercy and their manner of death was often particularly horrible; such was the revulsion and fear aroused by these formidable fighters.

Whilst most Ninja groups were shrouded in secrecy, the Iga and Koga camps became well known by reputation. Their members became the most highly paid of all the Ninja and were used on the most delicate assignments. Money was the motivating agent for the Ninja; they did not act for principles other than financial improvement. Such money as they earned was 'laundered' by investing it in honest merchant activities. By this means, the more successful clans were able to ensure their future operation.

2. JIU JITSU

'Jiu Jitsu', or 'Ju Jutsu' as it is alternatively known, means 'Compliant Techniques'. This is to say that the system yields to the force of an attack and having neutralised it, overcomes with an effective counter attack. The system is interesting because it is a 'Jitsu' form, i.e., one which depends simply upon the use of effective techniques, rather than serving other purposes. It is rather better known than other jitsu forms, being a system of combat that can be used or applied most effectively as the basis for present day self defence.

The earliest beginnings of Jiu Jitsu may be traced to strife-torn fifteenth and sixteenth century Japan. The warriors were generally clad in armour and always carried arms. When fighting with another armoured warrior, there was little point in using an unarmed system unless during the course of the combat, the two assailants had closed to such a distance that

A classic Jiu Jitsu throw using leverage applied to the opponent's elbow

sword play was impossible. At this stage, reliance on daggers would normally have taken over but there would have been times when it was desirable to capture, rather than despatch an enemy. Therefore methods were devised to exploit the joints in the armour to seize, hold and subdue the opponent so that he could be taken.

What unarmed moves were taught occurred in conjunction with armed combat only. At that time there was no need for a separate unarmed system and so one did not appear. The only evidence of continuing study showed itself in larger and larger numbers of these close quarter and unarmed techniques which came to be collectively known as 'Kumi-Uchi'.

In the Edo period, under the Tokugawa Shogunate, the opportunity for armed warfare was suppressed and the armoured warrior became obsolete. Kumi-Uchi had to change to meet new applications and techniques were devised for dealing with unarmoured assailants. These new forms were referred to specifically as 'Yawarra', 'Tai-Jitsu' and 'Jiu Jitsu'. In view of the current, albeit minimal involvement with weapons, their teachings remained unavailable to other than the warrior caste.

There is some evidence to suggest that Jiu Jitsu received an input from the martial art systems prevalent in the Southern part of China. This evidence is based upon the Japanese use of the term 'Kempo' ('Chuan'fa' in Chinese), which meant simply 'to fight with the fist'. In one case, it is recorded that a naturalised Japanese called Chin Gempin taught Chuan'fa techniques to selected students. If this is the case, then one must assume that these techniques were totally incorporated into the Japanese Ryu, or schools.

As the restriction upon the warrior caste continued, Jiu Jitsu schools opened which would teach common people. Because the latter were not allowed to carry arms, these schools used different methods from those which taught the warriors. To the consumer, denied access to classical martial art, Jiu Jitsu must have seemed to be the ideal way of learning how to deal with quarrelsome clients, or would-be muggers. This form of Jiu Jitsu became popular and the number of schools teaching it increased through the Edo period.

One of the most enlightened students of Jiu Jitsu was Jigoro Kano. Kano was a weak and sickly youth who took up Jiu Jitsu, joining the Tenjin Shinyo Ryu and the Kito Ryu. The former school was famous for its use of 'Atemi' – strikes at vulnerable parts of the opponent's body – and the latter for throwing techniques. He was so impressed by these studies that he went on to learn the classical Jiu Jitsu which had been taught to the warrior caste.

He was rather unhappy with the Japanese public's impressions of Jiu Jitsu – the art of the bully boy. He did not want his study to be associated with such goings on, and hence changed the name to Kodokan Judo. The term 'Judo' had been in previous use which is why he added the prefix 'Kodokan'. One of his ambitions was to return Jiu Jitsu to a position of respect and so he set about making his Kodokan Judo into an example for others to follow. One of the ways of achieving this was by encouraging sporting competition, with one competitor showing respect for the other. The effectiveness of his school was successfully tested against another Jiu Jitsu school.

Since its inception, Judo, like Karate, has placed a greater and greater emphasis on its sporting aspect. Kano wanted to retain some old techniques of Jiu Jitsu in his teachings and introduced kata for this purpose. He also brought in the concept of 'Randori', or 'free practice' which allows a free exchange of technique. This concept came from his study of the Kito Ryu Jiu Jitsu system.

Jiu Jitsu Techniques

In the present day, Jiu Jitsu has little connection with sport. There have been some attempts to hold national and international competitions but these have not received wide support. When they occur, they are rather like a Judo match, with some of the more dangerous Jiu Jitsu techniques removed for safety's sake. Yet another small scale attempt at producing a competition Jiu Jitsu format has resulted in the fighters using full contact boots and padded gloves that allow for grasping. In this latter form, kicks and punches are delivered with full force and when in close, grappling takes place. Such a bout can be won by a knockout, a submission, or rendering the opponent unconscious through a stranglehold.

Despite the failure of these attempts to create something that Jiu Jitsu is not, it remains an excellent form of self defence. The reason why it is so effective stems from the breadth of its syllabus. Its many techniques fit every situation likely to be encountered and so many alternative responses are available that any size or sex of person is accommodated.

Jiu Jitsu is based on the principles of harmony – just as in Aikido. If the opponent pulls the defender towards him, the defender obligingly pushes forwards; if the opponent pushes, the defender pulls. By this means, the defender is being compliant – agreeing with the force used against him, rather than fighting against it. It stands to reason that when force contests force, then the stronger will win. On the other hand, if force can be used to an advantage, then there is less possibility of losing on the grounds of physical weakness.

In a stalemate situation, where neither opponent is using force, then Jiu Jitsu can either initiate an attack, or respond to one. A diversionary move or strike is the best way to open an attack and for this purpose, Jiu Jitsu has retained the use of atemi. There are one or two latter day schools which have sought to specialise in atemi only. These sometimes call themselves 'Atemi Jitsu' or suchlike. When this occurs, it is an unnecessary further narrowing of a syllabus which is already depleted in the area of weapons training.

Atemi strikes tend to use the open hand, striking at a special point, rather than using a fist to club the area generally. Knife hand strikes are made to the throat, side or base of neck. Spearhand jabs – similar to those used in Karate – are aimed at the groin or eyes. Jiu Jitsu practitioners do use kicks, but these are seldom used above the level of the groin.

Having distracted the attacker with a strike, a hold or throw can be applied. When throwing the opponent, use can be made of hard surfaces to land him on. Keeping hold during the throw can either reduce the force of landings, or it can actually be used to ensure that the attacker unavoidably lands on his head, or tip of the shoulder.

At the completion of the throw, if the attacker has been held and not had the opportunity to roll away, a final lock can be applied. This lock is applied as often against the joint action, as with it. The object when applying a lock is to use the principle of leverage so that the amount of force applied is out of all proportion to the pain inflicted. To illustrate this concept, consider a simple thumb hold, by which the thumb is forcibly bent in its normal direction. The attacker uses the index finger to apply pressure at the thumb nail whilst his own thumb encircles the back of the attacked digit. Pressure on the attacked thumb nail causes considerable pain – sufficient to restrain most attackers, yet capable of being applied by a person of small build. The fingers are prime targets for the smaller person, since they require only a little force to cause pain.

The wrists are also used and a typical Jiu Jitsu wristlock

bends the forearm back upon itself, trapping the bent elbow inside the crook of the attacker's. The attacked wrist is bent forward in its normal direction of travel and the attacker's hands grasp the back of it at knuckle height, pulling it back towards the trapped elbow. This particular lock can be used on an attacker who has been thrown. The lock is applied and lifted, so the full weight of the prone body depends from the bent wrist.

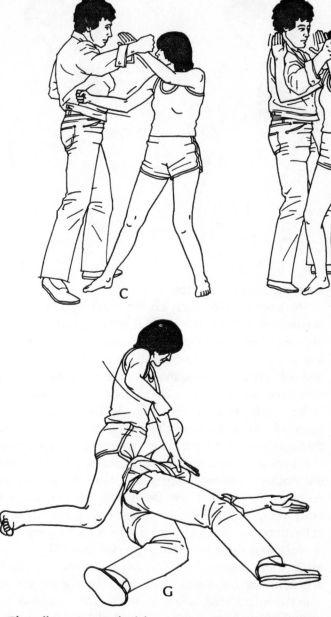

C

D

G

The attacker is about to throw a punch

The defender moves into the punch, interrupting it at source

An atemi strike to the ribs is used

The right hand slips up behind the attacker's punching arm and weight is transferred forwards

The defender insinuates her arm over the attacker's forearm and levers against his elbow

Twisting her hips and dropping, the elbow leverage is suddenly increased and the attacker has to go with the throw

The attacker is finished with a punch to the head

The elbow is attacked by moving it against its normal direction of movement. This joint is very often used in throws, such as that illustrated. The attacking arm is caught and the defender's right arm insinuates over the attacker's elbow, using the shoulder as leverage. When the defender steps to the side and applies pressure against the joint, the attacker is left with no other option than to go with the throw. The force of the throw is increased by the defender dropping down on one

The defender is held in a side head lock

A strike to the attacker's groin distracts him sufficiently to loosen his grip

Taking advantage of the loosened grip, both legs are seized

A butt to the stomach whilst pulling on the legs unbalances the attacker

Flat on his back, the attacker is finished off with a punch to the groin

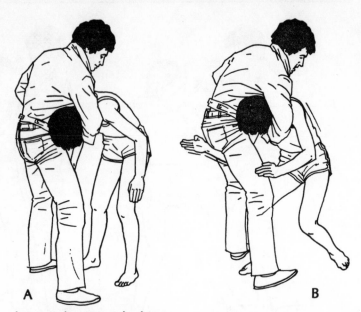

A   B

knee and twisting the hips.

This lowering of the body's centre of gravity during a throw is typical of Jiu Jitsu. The object is not to drag the opponent over but rather to weaken him with an atemi strike then drop low and come in from underneath, so that he is toppled over and onto his back. Some throws make use of the attacker's own force. As an example, the attacker lunges forward, only to be caught with an atemi blow to the throat, followed quickly by the defender seizing both his arms. The defender then puts one foot in the attacker's groin, or pit of stomach and rolls backwards onto the ground. By maintaining the grip on the attacker's arms and keeping the leg stiff, the attacker ends up being cartwheeled over the supine defender. As previously mentioned, the attacker is held onto during the whole of the throw, so that he lands on his head at its completion.

Blocking is also a part of the Jiu Jitsu syllabus and great use is made of the hook block. This curious move is powered by hip action, turning into the blow and catching it on the forearm, with the wrist turned outwards. The 'hook' so formed, prevents the blow from slipping past and, allied with a step into the attack, forms the basis for a subsequent grasp. The harder the opponent attacks, the harder the block and turn into it. By this means, the defender's force comes into harmony with that of the attacker and the latter can be thrown with little effort.

Evasions are also taught and these are almost always prefaced with an atemi strike. Consider the situation where an attacker has seized the head and is attempting to break the

C

D

E

neck with a sidewards twist. Before this can be applied, the defender strikes to the groin and then grabs a leg. A strong pull unbalances the attacker and natural self preservation causes him to release his weakened grip on the defender's head, so as to cushion his backwards fall.

On the floor, the defender can use a set defensive posture which brings the knee across the front of the stomach and a forearm across the face. When on the floor, the Jiu Jitsu exponent tries to keep turned towards the direction of attack and will sometimes counter by hooking one foot behind the attacker's leading leg and kicking at his kneecap with the other.

If someone is astride a supine defender and attempting to

strangle her, the defender can either attack the eyes, or face of the attacker and if these cannot be reached, attention can be switched to the groin which is conveniently close. A hard strike there can weaken the strangle to the extent that the elbows can be levered over, using a forearm bar and pressure. This causes the precarious attacker to overbalance.

In a second variety of this attack, the attacker is kneeling between the open legs of the supine victim. In this case, the victim insinuates her legs around the outside of the attacker's thighs and under his shins – using hooked feet for stability. A sudden extension of the defender's legs causes the attacker's to be suddenly shot backwards, collapsing him forwards. The forcibly arched back that this induces is exceedingly painful, allowing the victim to attack the eyes, or clap the open hands over the ears before rolling over onto the top and finishing

The attacker attempts to strangle his supine victim

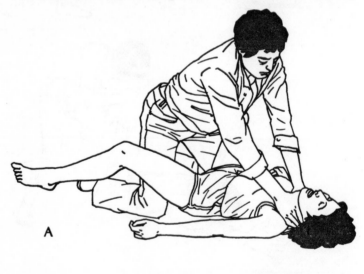

A

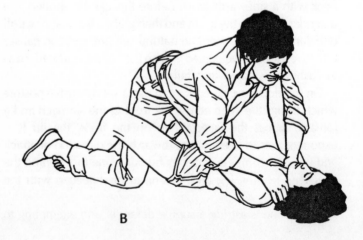

By means of an atemi strike with the fingers, the attacker is momentarily distracted whilst the victim insinuates her legs inside his

B

with an atemi blow to his exposed throat.

Not all Jiu Jitsu practice is unarmed. Use is made of the quarterstaff, the baton and the rice grinder handles ('Tonfa'). It is not known whether these have been latterly introduced, or whether they are a residue of practice from the Jiu Jitsu taught to the common people who had no access to weapons and therefore had to make do with weapons of convenience. The quarterstaff is around two metres in length and is made of polished Japanese oak. This is a formidable weapon, favoured by Buddhist monks and easily capable of keeping an armed assailant at bay. Not only could it be used to swing at attackers, it was also useful to jab with. An atemi like strike at the throat with the butt end could be quickly followed with a swinging strike at the head. A group of attackers could be dispersed by swinging it in wide arcs and even a mounted

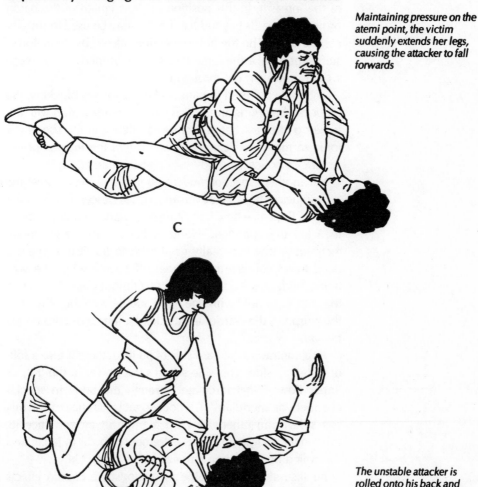

Maintaining pressure on the atemi point, the victim suddenly extends her legs, causing the attacker to fall forwards

C

The unstable attacker is rolled onto his back and finished with a punch

D

assailant brought down by using it to trip the horse. The disadvantage of this weapon is the amount of space needed to use it effectively.

The short baton, or club, is often used in the Jiu Jitsu dojo. This is less effective with multiple attackers but it may be used where space is at a premium. Many people consider that the baton has only one use — that of clubbing at the head or limbs. This is not the case, however, and it is frequently used to jab, to apply a strangle, or to trap a grasping hand. The Japanese police are experts in the use of the staff and the club and have created a system specially concerned with their use.

The tonfa is a favourite weapon of some Jiu Jitsu schools. It consists of a length of flattened hard wood baton, from which projects at right angles a peg. In normal use, the user holds the weapon by the peg, with the baton lying along the underside of the forearm. In this position, a short length of the baton projects forwards beyond the fist and may be used to supplement a blow. The forearm protection offered by the baton is sufficient to take the force of a staff. A properly used sword would, however, cut through it.

The tonfa are used in pairs and whilst one is blocking, the other can be swung around, giving a clubbing action with the longer part of the baton. Renewed interest in the use of the tonfa in many Jiu Jitsu dojos has caught the interest of the American police who now use clubs patterned on it.

Yet another aspect of modern Jiu Jitsu training involves the techniques of tying an adversary. This is descended from the times of Bujitsu, where it became necessary to capture, rather than kill the opponent. Hand in hand with the grappling techniques that eventually gave birth to Jiu Jitsu, came the need to immobilise the prisoner effectively whilst he was being held. This led to a series of techniques which allowed the warrior to hold with one hand and tie with the other. For this purpose, the warrior always kept a length of cord on his person.

As a contrast to the hard side of Jiu Jitsu, there is also a soft, or 'internal' side. This side stresses the power of the 'Ki', or 'Inner Power' that circulates through the body in special channels, or 'meridians'. It is not altogether strange to find this soft side in an otherwise hard martial art aspect since its forerunner Aiki-Jiu Jitsu, was extremely popular in Japan and this relied heavily upon harnessing the body's ki.

Jiu Jitsu students are able to demonstrate certain effects caused by the channelling of ki energy. One such demonstrates how a heavy blow can be taken on the stomach, without any apparent effect. To be sure, other 'Hard' systems can demonstrate the same thing, but these depend upon the sudden contraction of the stomach muscles. Provided that air is held above the diaphragm and expelled suddenly, the stomach can take quite a severe impact without injury. The difference with the soft system in Jiu Jitsu is that the stomach remains relaxed. The advantage of this is that there is no chance of being caught unawares with the stomach muscles unready. When a student of the hard system is caught thus, the blow often does have an effect. Other Jiu Jitsu students are able to demonstrate their ability to withstand kicks in the groin by harnessing ki force. Still others are able to take full power blows to the neck and throat.

Jiu Jitsu and self defence
It is a regrettable fact that in today's society, there remains a need for individuals to be able to defend themselves. This applies to males and females alike, for more common than sexual assaults on females is the simple act of gratuitous violence which can follow an evening's entertainment at a pub or disco. There are many instances also of people being attacked in their own homes and some even in their cars. In all cases, the self defence response must conform with the requirements of the Law.

The Law basically says that a person must use only such force as is necessary to nullify an attack. The important word here is 'nullify'. This simply means, to render the attacker ineffective. What it does not mean, is using an excess of force, with or without a weapon, to maim or kill the attacker.

It goes without saying that the force needed to nullify an attack will be related to the force and nature of the attack itself. In the simplest sense, this means that when fending off a ten-year-old child, one does not use the same force as would be required against a 225 pound body builder. This is where the flexible response of Jiu Jitsu is so useful. Its techniques are more useable in a wider range of situations than those of a purely striking system. It is possible, using Jiu Jitsu, to restrain a person without injury and that is why the art is often used as the basis for Police self defence systems.

Being concerned only with the effectiveness of the technique, Jiu Jitsu scores significantly over the do martial art ways. On the other hand, the sheer size of the Jiu Jitsu syllabus is such that it takes many years to master. In any attack

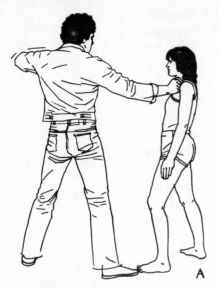

A

B

The attacker seizes his victim and makes ready to strike her

The victim diverts the attacker with a strike to the throat. His other hand is trapped against the victim's shoulder

situation, the victim must be able to respond very quickly indeed and delay can cause the circumstances of the attack to change. This means that an assailant may grab the jacket lapel and a response should be made at that point, simply because the next stage of the attack may be to punch the victim in the face. It is no use wondering what to do with the lapel hold once the punch lands! There is regrettably no short cut to skill and the person who feels the need to acquire a real competence in self defence must face the fact that he or she has several years of intensive study ahead of them. Many short courses of self defence cannot hope to cover enough attack responses to be learned in the short time they allow.

On the other hand, too many schools of self defence recommend using techniques, such as high kicks, which require loose clothes. Fortunately, Jiu Jitsu does not require the wearing of any special clothes to make its techniques effective. Still other self defence courses teach techniques which require great physical agility or strength. Jiu Jitsu, with its compliant techniques demands neither.

Many self defence courses teach a response to a knife attack but in most cases, the knife attack as shown is totally artificial. This is easy to recognise in that the attacker usually lunges forward, with the blade held in the leading hand. The knife is obligingly held out for the demonstrator to perform a whole series of spectacular but unlikely counters. In reality, the knife is held in the rear hand where it is used to slash. The front hand

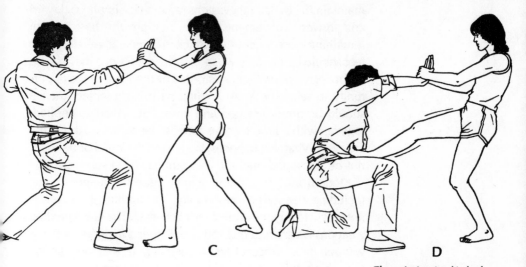

C

D

The wrist is seized in both hands, is twisted and forced upwards, bringing the attacker to his knees

A kick in the groin completes the sequence

is used to grab the victim.

Used expertly, a knife is almost impossible to catch when being waved about. Any attempt to do so is very likely to cause severe injury to the hand. The best thing to do is simply escape, if that is at all possible. If the attacker is after money, then this must be given over promptly. Only under circumstances where the victim has little doubt that he is about to be knifed, should any form of defence be attempted.

Obviously, the first thing to be considered is that of distance. It is very important to try to remain away from the range of the knife, or the grasping hand. If it is possible to keep a little distance, then the likelihood of escaping uninjured is improved. In the street, care must be taken not to let oneself be backed into a corner, or against a wall. In any sudden confrontation with an armed assailant, there will simply not be the opportunity to reach down and slip off the shoe (which may be a lace up), or to take off a jacket and wrap it around the forearm.

If distance is not available and there is nothing that can be quickly used as a weapon – such as a chair, or a dustbin lid, or even a handful of gravel – then all that can be done is an atemi strike to the attacker's front knee followed by a fast jab at the eyes, using open fingers. Whilst a strong attacker may be able to take a kick in the groin, or a strike at the neck, few people can ignore damage to the eyes. Any attack to the eyes however, must be restricted to possible life or death situations.

Where distance is available, every move should be made to maintain it. Use lateral evasions rather than simple backward and forward movements, since they are the best way of remaining close for counter attack in comparative safety. The feet should be the only weapons employed since they have a slight degree of protection afforded by the shoes. If the opportunity to seize the knife holding wrist is presented, then it should be firmly grasped and immediate leverage applied, together with a simultaneous atemi strike, to try and throw the attacker. Whatever happens, the grip on the knifehand should not be slackened until the assailant has been subdued.

Modern Jiu Jitsu training actually teaches weapon usage, including weapons of opportunity. This training, however, is not taught to anyone under black belt level. The law regarding weapons is very rigorous and people found in possession of a weapon face prosecution. Remember, a weapon can be something quite harmless in itself — it does not have to be a dagger, or a switchblade. For instance, it is quite legal to be carrying a brick if building a house but not if going to a soccer match!

Jiu Jitsu stresses the value of weapons of opportunity which may be used in cases of extreme danger only. A dustbin lid not only makes a shield, it is quite an effective discus or club. A handful of sand, or gravel thrown into the face makes a good substitute for atemi. When selecting the weapon to be used, it is important to take into account the surroundings. If attacked in the entrance hall of a house, a broom is not a good weapon of opportunity because it is too long and tends to catch in things.

3. AIKIDO

The name 'Aikido' means 'The Way of Harmony'. It is a martial art 'way' founded by Morihei Ueshiba, a farmer's son. Ueshiba is reputed to have been a strong young man with a deep interest in the martial arts. So great was his interest that he left the family farm and travelled to Tokyo, to join the Tenjin Shinyo Ryu of Tozawa Tokusaburo. He was subsequently conscripted into the Japanese Army and served in the Russo–Japanese War. It is said that this afforded him the opportunity to observe other forms of martial art. He continued to study and practise hard during his conscription and eventually became a teacher of his Ryu.

Following demobilisation, he decided to return to the land but ended up enrolling in a Jiu Jitsu school under the direction of Sokaku Takeda. Takeda was an expert in Kenjitsu and had trained under Saigo Tanomo of the Aizu warrior clan. The latter were slow to lose their martial arts ability under the restrictions imposed by the Shogunate and continued to maintain a high standard of bujitsu training. As part of their training syllabus, unarmed combat was taught and this was known as 'Oshikiuchi'.

Takeda was much taken with Oshikiuchi, adapting and changing it to his own ideas for self defence. So successful was

Akido techniques rely on using the attacker's violence against him

his modification, which he called 'Daito Ryu Jiu Jitsu', that he was asked to teach it to the Hokkaido Police Force. It was whilst he was teaching there that the young Ueshiba came to him.

Ueshiba trained hard and soon reached the rank of teacher. At this time, a further change in name produced the now familiar title of 'Daito Ryu Aiki Jiu Jitsu'. The concept of the 'Ki', or 'Inner Power' was very much in fashion at the time and a great many books had been written about it. It is open to comment whether the inclusion of 'Aiki' in the title signified any great change in the system, or whether it was merely an early exercise in marketing.

Ueshiba became dissatisfied with the teaching of techniques solely for effect, for not only was he a keen martial artist, he was also very religious. He became more concerned with the 'Do' side of the martial art — that which uses the practice of techniques to assist the mind and body to develop. He therefore founded 'Aikido' and was probably pleased to see it become quickly accepted, gaining more members and support than the still continuing original school of Aiki Jiu Jitsu.

Being a strong martial artist, Ueshiba was extremely forceful in his earlier Aikido practice. He was, however, preoccupied with the concept of using the attacker's strength against him after initially weakening the attack with a skillfully applied atemi strike to a weak point. From this stage onwards, the attacker's force was redirected under the control of the defender.

The art of Aikido, coming as it did from Jiu Jitsu, relied upon grappling to subdue an opponent. Strikes, when taught, were of a distracting, or weakening nature and were incidental to the main target of the attack — which was generally a joint such as that of the wrist.

Therefore, in a typical Aikido response to attack, the defender will wait for the attacker to move into his sphere of influence. A person throwing a punch will be encouraged to overextend, usually by the defender's use of distance. When this happens, the defender quickly evades the punch with a hiptwist and seizes the extended fist before it can be withdrawn. Once seized, the wrist is painfully twisted in such a way as to either bring the attacker to his knees, or to throw him.

The redirection of the attacker's vigour is the basis of Aikido practice. In effect, the defender harmonises with his attacker and then uses this harmony to overcome rather like throwing a

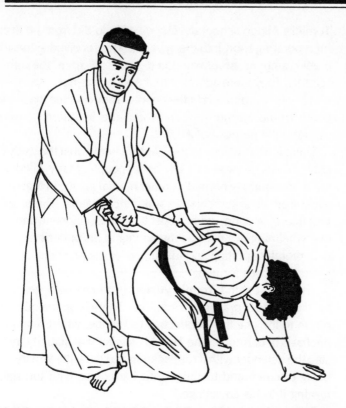

An elbow lock applies pressure against the normal direction of movement

brick at a curtain. The fabric of the curtain yields under the impact but in so doing, it deprives the thrown brick of its force and causes it to fall, spent of all energy.

Though this idea remained the basis of Aikido, the methods of practice gradually changed and it became less and less necessary to practise on a genuine attack. Nowadays, the would-be attacker runs forward with the arm to be attacked obligingly held out from the body. Watching two skilled Aikidoka (Aikido practitioners) training impresses the onlooker with the grace and ballet-like fluidity of the art. The split skirts, traditionally worn by the higher grades, enhance the smooth swirl of movement as the pseudo attack is taken gracefully and drawn out into a long twisting throw or hold. The culmination is often a symbolic strike to a weak point; all that remains of the original atemi.

Schools

Some of Ueshiba's earlier students evidently did not agree with the way Aikido was going. The gradual loss of effective techniques and their substitution with ones which were nice looking but ineffective, caused a number to found their own schools. One such school was that of the late Kenji Tomiki.

Tomiki's Aikido school developed as Judo did from Jiu Jitsu, incorporating sport into the syllabus. This received a considerable amount of unwarranted criticism from the other schools. They were adamant that Aikido was not a sport – it was a way of producing better people. They claimed that there could be no harmony in sport and the inclusion of rules defeated the purpose of Aikido.

There is no evidence in the Western world, that the study of classical Aikido produces any better people. Many Aikidoka are as disarmingly normal as other martial artists, in that they suffer from an argumentative and critical nature. The proper practice of a sport, with respect for the opponent and no overwhelming desire to be the winner at his or her expense, is as morally uplifting and instructive as the practice of gymnastic exercises for two!

The idea behind Tomiki Aikido is to strive to generate harmony under practical conditions. There is an intention to return to the practice of effective technique, whilst retaining the basis of harmony. The Tomiki attacker will actually try to stab the defender with a rubber knife and the latter will try, by using distance and technique, to harmonise with the stab, turning it to his advantage.

Tomiki Aikido also uses an unarmed one-to-one and an even more frantic two-to-one form of combat. The latter in particular, requires a great deal of skill, with one attacker frequently being thrown into the path of the other in order to gain time and/or space. A true master of Tomiki Aikido practising under these conditions reflects the true nature of Aikido – that of being in harmony with the forces within and without.

Gozo Shioda was another senior student of the master, who left to pursue his own ideas. As with the Tomiki School, the Yoshinkan preaches the importance of ki and in a way similar to Tomiki, they test its effectiveness by expecting the attacker to come in hard. Yoshinkan Aikido is concerned with effectiveness of Aikido technique and so is used to train units of the Japanese police force.

Yoshinkan is one of those schools which study the effective use of atemi strikes to the more vulnerable parts of the attacker's anatomy. An example of this is the backfist to the eyes which is frequently used to divert attention from a lock. The training of Yoshinkan aims towards a self defence regime and the high grades are quick at countering even the fastest of punches. The principle of effective distance is allied with evasive movements so performed as to cause the attack to

A

B

C

The attacker holds the knife concealed

A lunge with the knife is avoided using body movement and the wrist is grasped

The captured wrist is twisted and the knife brought to the attacker's own throat

miss by the minimum effective distance. This allows the aikidoka to remain close by, but safe from the attacker.

Another of Ueshiba's students to set up his own school was Koichi Tohei. Tohei became interested in using Aikido to develop ki. Someone who is able to harness ki is seen to possess great strength, immovability and balance. They are reputedly able to strike effectively, yet without apparently using great muscular force. In Aikido, the masters of ki can cause someone to be thrown through the air by the force of their own movement alone.

There are many so called examples of ki which are no more than simple tricks. Consider, for instance, the so called 'unbendable arm' of Aikido. This is demonstrated by high grades and is used to show ki developed through proper practice.

To show 'unbendable arm', the demonstrator rests his relaxed lower arm on a student's shoulder. He tells the student that he is not using ki and invites him to pull down upon his elbow joint with both hands. Under these conditions, the demonstrator's arm bends easily. Then he tells the student that he is going to use ki and invites him once again to pull down. This time, the student is unable to bend the arm, even though

The application of proper leverage has spectacular results

it is clearly relaxed. The demonstrator often explains that he does this by 'visualising the flow of ki to be like water from a hosepipe, streaming down the arm and spraying out from the fingers'. What he does not explain is that in this second case, he merely pushes his arm over the student's shoulder as the latter is straining away. The effect of this is to make the student work against himself! No matter how hard he strains, that relaxed arm cannot be bent.

Techniques of Aikido
The practice of Aikido takes place in the 'Dojo', or 'Place of the Way'. The traditional Aikido dojo reflects the Japanese character, having a quiet, rustic simplicity. Wherever possible, natural materials are used and the authentic dojo will have the same temperature as the outside climate. The floor is generally matted, since the practice of Aikido involves throws. The way that the aikidoka lands from a throw is quite distinct. Unlike the follower of Judo, the aikidoka does not slap the floor with his arm as he breakfalls; he simply rolls out of the throw.

To practice a roll out, the student literally dives onto the floor, extending the forward arm to make first contact. The arm is kept out and slightly curved, so that the aikidoka turns forward movement into a roll onto the back. To prevent injury, the spine is curved and the head well tucked in. As the roll continues to the point where he is coming up onto his backside, the legs (which are folded beneath) take over and bring him into a standing, ready stance. The roll out may also be performed when falling backwards.

As the student becomes more and more confident, the dives can be extended into leaps of great height and distance. In some schools, the students are encouraged to jump high over the backs of others, landing quite forcefully in the process. As long as the roll out is properly executed, the whole thing is relatively painless.

The gi worn by aikidoka may either be the heavy white weave of the judo jacket, with white cotton trousers, or it may be the altogether lighter gi of the karateka. The latter is quite suitable since Aikido does not involve as much use of the gi in the execution of its techniques. Aikido uses a system of coloured belts which denote progression in personal ability. The number and colours of these belts vary according to the school of Aikido practised. As in other martial art ways, the black belt with the included Dan stages represents the

A

B

C

D

E

Fall forward with an outstretched and bent arm

Take the fall on the bent arm and begin to roll in the direction of the fall. Roll onto your back

The momentum must be maintained so that you continue rolling and gather your legs up under you

Stand up smoothly, all in one go

best of technical proficiency.

The exercises which precede the Aikido class serve to loosen the joints and in particular, the wrists. During the course of training, the wrists will be seized and twisted quite a lot, so it is not unusual to go home with them sore or aching. With regular training, this soon passes and the wrists become supple. A supple wrist is able to bend with applied force and this bending induces less pain than in the unconditioned limb. For this reason, many high grades in Aikido cannot be hurt by a wrist hold.

The attacker seizes the jacket. Distract him with a sudden strike to the face

Seize his hand from above with your right hand and twist his wrist. Use the left hand to hold his wrist

Press down and twist with the left hand, using the right to keep his wrist painfully twisted

After practising roll outs and exercises, the class moves on to deal with the basic locks, holds and throws that make up the syllabus of basic Aikido techniques. The way the class is run is

The attacker seizes the jacket and is distracted with a backfist strike. Your right hand grasps his wrist from underneath

Simultaneously twist his wrist and strike him with your elbow as you duck under his lifted arms

Raise the captured arm up against the elbow whilst twisting the wrist

typically Japanese in the quiet discipline and respect shown at all times. The instructor demonstrates the technique to be practised and the students set to in pairs.

A typical basic technique involves one student grabbing the other by the collar of his tunic. The defender responds by simultaneously striking at his attacker's eyes with one hand and grasping the lapel-holding hand in an overarm grasp with the other. The thumb points back to the defender and his attacking fingers curl over the little finger edge of the attacker's palm. This edge is rotated upwards by pulling with the fingers and pressing down with the thumb side of the palm. Having administered the strike at the eyes, the other hand now loops over the top and grasps the attacker's elbow. Pressure is applied downwards on the elbow whilst the wrist is turned upwards. The result of this is to force the attacker quickly to his knees.

When an excess of pressure is being put on the trapped joint, the student can indicate submission by means of a slap against his own thigh. This is the signal for the attacker to release pressure immediately. In all grasps, the lower fingers only are used to make the hold and frequently the index finger is seen to be pointing.

To practise another hold, the attacker seizes the defender in a rear bear hug, trapping the arms against the body. The defender replies with an atemi strike to the attacker's groin, which causes him to loosen his grip slightly. This is sufficient for the defender to seize the attacker's left wrist, whilst ducking under the arm. To assist this very fast move, the captured wrist is rotated and lifted, causing pain. To discourage the attacker from re-using his right hand, strike can be delivered on the way under the lifted joint. Once underneath, the defender's second hand is used to reinforce the lifting, twisting pressure that is being applied to the wrist joint. This has the effect of bringing the attacker onto his toes.

As the pain becomes unbearable, the attacker will slap his thigh and the pressure is eased. Maintaining the hold, the erstwhile attacker may now be steered around the mat at will and at any stage the grip may be altered. By maintaining the wrist hold whilst using the other hand to pull back on the elevated elbow, the attacker's arm may be brought down inside the defender's. The defender's elbow abuts against the rear of the attacker's and only one hand is thereafter needed to keep his open hand bent forward at the wrist, so its fingertips are pointing towards the floor.

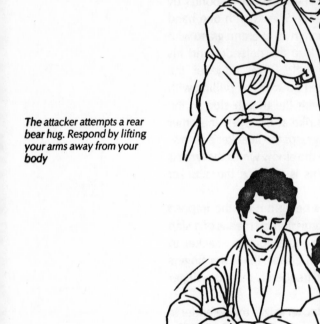

The attacker attempts a rear bear hug. Respond by lifting your arms away from your body

Step to the right and drive off his right hand. Take his left wrist in yours

Even attackers with strong wrists may be subdued with this hold, since it can be varied in power simply by sliding the applying fingers further down the hand, towards the knuckles.

A very simple move, typical of Aikido, involves a diagonal forward sidestep as the attacker moves strongly forward. In this way, the defender positions immediately behind the would-be attacker's back. From here, the defender simply places both hands on the attacker's shoulders and pulls him sharply backwards and downwards so that he falls to the floor.

More advanced students go on to practise responses to faster attacks. One will throw a fast punch at the other's face, only to have him step to the side and seize the incoming fist with both hands. One hand forms a knife edge pressed against the side of the wrist whilst the other applies a painful twist. Coupled to this is a drawing up and around of the helpless

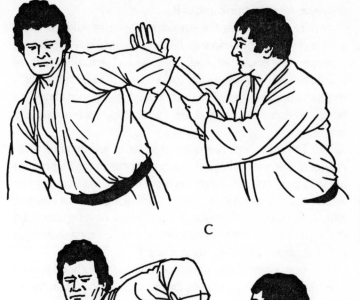

C

Pull the hand under his held arm and then hit the back of his elbow forcing him forward and down to the floor

D

Alternatively, after you step through, seize his wrist with your other hand; then lift and twist it

attacker. A sudden deep sidestep results in the attacker being hurled over onto his back. Through this, the wrist hold is maintained; the victim's arm is extended and pulled out, so that he is forced onto his face. The extended arm is then held by kneeling on the elbow joint whilst a token atemi blow is aimed at the back of the neck.

In Tomiki dojos, there is also training in the tactics of competition. Rubber knives are produced and opponents practise evading stabs and applying counters. Aikido kata is also practised. This is a series of moves where the attack and its defence are prearranged by the partners to produce a smooth performance. The kata is at the heart of Aikido training and practised properly, it promotes an understanding of the art. When the techniques and movements of Aikido are mastered, then the mind is left free to take action without the delaying need to think about it.

Kenjitsu techniques are sometimes seen in Aikido. There are katas which show how to disarm a swordsman but there is considerable doubt whether they would actually work in practice. Use is made of the oaken sword to develop wrist strength and flexibility. The student holds the sword above his head and repeatedly cuts downwards, stopping abruptly at a set point.

The Tomiki school has originated some self defence techniques of interest to the police forces. Some of the techniques are very practical, whilst others involving the disarming of an armed attacker are not. A person holding a gun has a weapon which can kill at a distance. It is therefore never guaranteed that such an attacker will stand close enough for a technique to be applied before the trigger can be pulled.

The best systems are developed through study of several alternatives and it has never been unusual for a teacher to study more than one system. By this means, the techniques of one art can be used to improve the performance of another. A recent example of this came during a training seminar when an aikidoka was able to suggest an alternative wrist hold to a karateka who had need of one in a particular form. The Aikido alternative was much better than that originally taught in the Karate school.

4. KARATE

Introduction

The term 'Karate-do' nowadays means 'The Way of the Empty Hand.' Since its early and secret beginnings, it has mushroomed out throughout the world, becoming a well organised and popular activity. The world Karate governing body is known as 'The World Union of Karate-do Organisations', or 'WUKO' for short.

One of the main reasons for Karate's rapid expansion in the Western world has been the successful development of 'Sport Karate' which allows Karate practitioners (or 'Karateka' to give them their proper name) to compete in national and international competitions. Although sport karate is really only a small part of Karate-do, it has come to be regarded as its

A stance from the Karate Kata 'Sochin'

major manifestation. This has had an adverse effect upon the study and upon the nature of the art itself. On the other hand, were not sport karate so successful, then the Way of the Empty Hand would have far less people studying it throughout the world.

Time and time again in the martial arts, there has been a dramatic change in the old martial art when sporting aspects are introduced. Techniques are reviewed in the light of the sporting arena and new strategies devised to take advantage of the rules of competiton. As a result, there is often a drift away from the original concepts.

Perhaps the most significant change in Karate-do came when the art was introduced to Japan in the early twentieth century by the scholarly Gichin Funakoshi. Funakoshi may have seen the way that Judo had been so readily accepted by the educational system of Japan and visualised Karate-do achieving the same success. The teaching of Karate-do to a large class probably itself led to a change in the art, since this would have been a major departure from the old way of teaching one or two carefully selected students.

When teaching a large class of students, therefore, movements have to be broken up into a series which is easily understood. Actions which were previously performed simultaneously might have to be taught as two separate moves to assist their learning.

After the Second World War, Karate-do was not recognised by the Americans as a combat system. Consequently it escaped the prohibition placed on other suchlike activities and came to be taught to Westerners. The American soldiers no doubt found Karate-do rather easier to learn than the more flowing Aikido, precisely because of the breakdown of the movements. The existence of lifelike pre-arranged sparring and the eventual appearance of sport karate all added to its popularity, so that it is now one of the world's best known arts.

Nowadays, many karateka drop the 'do' from the title and call it just 'Karate'.

History

Karate comes from Okinawa, one of the Ryukyu islands that form the chain of 'stepping stones' between Japan and China. Because of their position midway between the two, it was here that the cultures of Japan and China met and mingled. The native Okinawans were pawns in a political machine and from time to time their island was overrun by occupying

Japanese forces. The Japanese overlords forbade Okinawans the right to carry weapons. This was a normal practice for the Japanese, who operated a rigid caste structure in which only the warriors were permitted to bear arms.

Also in Okinawa were military and cultural missions from China. These occupied set areas, collectively known as 'The Nine Villages'. From time to time, members of these missions could be persuaded to give demonstrations of Chinese martial arts to the populace. From these demonstrations, techniques and concepts were analysed by the Okinawans who added them to their own native system. Two Chinese military attaches whose names have come down to the present day are Chinto and Waishinzan (the Japanese rendering of their names). The former is remembered by having a Karate kata named after him. Some sources also refer to a Chinese visitor named Ku Shanku and, if he did exist, it is interesting to speculate whether he contributed anything to the other Karate kata of the same name.

A second way of introducing new techniques might well have been via the large numbers of foreign sailors that docked at Okinawa. There is some evidence that these introduced some new weapons techniques and perhaps even the weapons themselves.

There arose three main schools of Okinawan martial art based upon the main areas of population. These were known as Naha-te, Shuri-te and Tomari-te. The suffix 'Te' incidentally, means 'hand' and a way of referring to all three schools was to call them simply 'Okinawa-te', or 'Hand of Okinawa'. There were various other names used at different stages of development and generally these all used the word 'hand'.

Despite the veil of secrecy drawn over the study of Okinawan Hand, various rumours began circulating about the exploits of certain masters. One, it was said, had perfected the claw-hand technique to such a degree that he could strip the bark from a tree in a matter of seconds. Another was said to be able to punch so hard that he could bury his fist as far as the forearm in hard ground! One of the renowned early masters of Okinawan Hand was 'Karate' Sakugawa. This first use of the term 'Karate' is interesting, though in this case it meant 'Chinese Hand'.

The extent to which the Chinese arts affected the Okinawan forms cannot now be accurately judged but it is certain that there was a measurable effect. Well into the late nineteenth and early twentieth century, Okinawan masters were travelling to the Chinese mainland to continue their studies and a careful study of the modern Okinawan based Karate reveals a number of similarities with Southern Chinese Shaolin systems. To be fair, however, it is important to point out that the number of things one can do using the hands and feet as weapons, is limited and so there are bound to be similarities which are not based upon a common origin.

Regardless of where the actual techniques came from, there was great interest in the study of the Okinawa Hand and not unnaturally, such interest leaked back to the Japanese over-lords. The Japanese navy was particularly interested in Okinawa-te and contacted one practitioner, a mild man-nered, scholarly poet/school teacher named Gichin Funakoshi. He was prevailed upon to give a display and so impressed the visiting admirals that they secured a subsequent demonstration from Funakoshi, this time in front of the Emperor of Japan.

It is evident from this, that at the turn of the century, the Japanese attitude towards Okinawans studying martial arts had become more liberal. From his writings, Funakoshi appeared totally loyal to the Emperor and was clearly not the type one would have imagined disobeying imperial edicts. Japan was moving with colossal speed into the twentieth century and many old values, prohibitions and laws were swept aside.

Funakoshi was well received in Japan and there set up the first Karate training school, or 'Dojo'. This was known as the 'Shotokan', or 'Shoto's Club'. The word 'Shoto' was Funakoshi's pen-name that he used when writing poetry. Being translated, it means 'Waving Pines'.

At first, Funakoshi referred to his art as Ryukyu Kempo ('Okinawan Way of the Fist'). This may well have caused some confusion since there was already a 'Kempo' in exist-ence in Japan at that time. The Japanese Kempo was in some ways similar to the Okinawan variety, concentrating upon the use of blows and kicks to injure an opponent. It was one of the branches of Jiu Jitsu and because of its effectiveness, study of it was suppressed by the Japanese government. This might well have influenced Funakoshi into adopting the name 'Karate-do' ('Way of the Chinese Hand').

At that time, Jigoro Kano had devised Judo – 'The Compliant Way' – also from the ancient Japanese art of Jiu Jitsu. Having noted the fate of Japanese Kempo and the popu-larity of Judo, it is a possibility that Funakoshi decided upon a development of the Okinawan martial art taught to him by Masters Azato and Itosu, moving away from the dangerous techniques and towards a form more acceptable to the Japanese authorities.

In Japan during the period before the outbreak of the Second World War, an anti-Chinese atmosphere began developing and by a neat change in calligraphy, the pictogram for Karate-do, The Way of the China Hand, became Karate-do, The Way of the Empty Hand. Together with this alteration came many other changes in technique names with the syllabus taking on a decidedly Japanese appearance. In order to teach the larger classes, the previously described methods had to be used, with the result that Funakoshi's Karate-do moved quite a way from the art he was taught.

Below: Karate uses a great deal of muscle power in technique delivery. A shout, or 'Kiai' is used to focus power

Left: The axe kick is a particularly strong technique, impacting as it does with the full weight of the leg

Assisting Funakoshi with the development of Karate-do were his two sons, Yoshitake ('Gigo') and Yoshihide. The basic stances from which the Karate techniques were practised became lower and lower and the semi-circular forward step was abandoned in the search for a more rapid movement. The form of the front fist altered and the front kick came to be practised with the ball of the foot, rather than with the toes pulled downwards.

Some of these later changes contrasted sharply with Funakoshi's original methods. He still practised with a long wooden staff – known as a 'Bo' and many movements of his school were based upon its use. He described how, when forced to fight as a last resort, might was no match for skill. He explained how an old man, when faced with a young would-be mugger, stepped inside the younger man's attack and seized his testicles!

Despite this clear example of effective Karate, his school continued to concentrate upon the breaking up of movements into easily learnt sequences and some of his senior students began to feel that much of the original Karate had been lost. As a result of this the Japan Karate Association, which had grown from the Shotokan, lost a number of its most senior instructors. These instructors formed the Shotokai, or 'Shoto's Way', a body dedicated to amateur principles.

Funakoshi's hold over Karate-do was perhaps loosening slightly as he got older. Always aware of the dangers of the original Okinawan martial art, he forbade free sparring (where two opponents actually fight each other but using 'muted' techniques). This ban was not observed and informal, bloody sparring between different schools of Karate continued unabated whilst the senior students of Funakoshi worked on ever faster forms of pre-arranged sparring, culminating in a syllabus requirement to free fight for the black belt examination! This was another milestone in the development of Karate-do.

Funakoshi believed that katas were the only way that Karate-do techniques could be performed properly and though he had moved a great way from his original practice, he nevertheless still regarded it as being a true fighting art, whereas his students were becoming preoccupied with the idea of testing Karate-do techniques by means of sparring. Quite clearly, some sort of rules had to be devised and in so doing, Karate-do took a further step away from the original effective system.

The Schools of Karate

The rapid establishment of Funakoshi's new Karate-do had a profound influence upon the development of other schools. Though Funakoshi was an innovator, he was by no means the only Karate teacher of the time. Indeed, his master Itosu had also taught the well respected Kannryo Higaonna of the Naha-te school. Higaonna in turn, produced two well-known students – Chojun Miyagi of the Goju Ryu school and Kenwa Mabuni of the Shito Ryu.

Chojun Miyagi came to Japan and began teaching his style of Karate not long after Funakoshi. One of Miyagi's best known Japanese students was Gogen Yamaguchi, the Founder of the Japanese Goju Kai. After teaching for a while in Japan and Okinawa, Miyagi visited the Chinese mainland and there studied Chinese boxing methods, especially those of the Pa Kua school. When he returned to Okinawa, he re-drafted his Goju Ryu school to fit in with the techniques he had recently learnt.

The result of this was two styles of Goju – the 'new post-China Goju' as taught in Okinawa and the original Goju as taught in Japan by his senior student there, Yamaguchi. This change in approach is quite common, not only in Karate schools but also in other martial arts. In at least one case, the master gradually changed his martial art way as he grew older and less supple. A lot of his younger students preferred the original, more vigorous form and so left to pursue it.

The division within the Goju school continued until comparatively recently when the present day masters of the two branches met and decided to reunite. Miyagi's student Miyasato taught the well-known Morihei Higaonna, whilst Yamaguchi taught his son, Goshi.

The term 'Goju' means 'Hard/Soft' and it refers to the way in which the style counters a hard attack with a soft defence and a soft attack with a hard response. The original Goju was extremely hard and put great emphasis on the use of the stance known as 'Sanchin'. In this stance, the hips are pushed forward, the line of the feet converges and the knees are rotated outward. The result of holding it properly for any length of time is total fatigue, not helped by the teacher 'testing' the stance, to see whether the body is sufficiently rigid. Testing takes the form of a series of kicks and punches applied liberally to the subject's anatomy. Nowhere is sacred and even hard kicks between the legs must be tolerated impassively! This latter is not as terrible as it sounds, since if the stance is properly formed, then thrusting the hips forwards and up pulls the genitals up from between the legs and out of harm's way.

The theory is that sanchin stance promotes great strength and immovability. Those who have practised it certainly do seem to be extraordinarily strong. The flexing and sustained tension of the muscles involved are surely the forerunners of Mr. Charles Atlas' theory of Dynamic Tension. Indeed, so hard do the muscles work against each other in sanchin, that students practising it sometimes placed a coin between the cheeks of their backsides and then moved from stance to stance without once dropping it!

Needless to say, such powerful movements are not suited to sport karate and one seldom finds Goju practitioners indulging in it. Also the school does not go in for the cultivation of what is called focus, or 'Kime' to the same extent as others. Many of the techniques are circular in their delivery path and lack the pretty looking snappy movements of other styles.

Sanchin stance is an extremely strong stance. It forms the basis for many Okinawan schools of Karate

Goju Ryu Karate makes great use of its own peculiar form of weight training

A final interesting point about Goju is the use of weights to supplement training. The Goju school uses lollipop-like strength stones and these are held in the hand and moved through the air in a series of blocking and striking techniques. There are also large earthenware urns full of stones that Goju karateka grasp, lift and move about. There is the story about a world class sport-karate man watching Higaonna casually moving two of these urns about as he chatted to his visitors. The watching karateka went over when the group had moved away and tried to lift one of the urns. When his efforts with one hand failed, he crouched down low and embraced the urns with both arms. It was only then that he could lift the one!

Funakoshi's Master Itosu also taught Kenwa Mabuni, in addition to the latter's instruction by Kannryo Higaonna. As a result of this distinguished guidance, Mabuni originated a style which he first called Hanko Ryu, or 'Half Hard Way'. Quite obviously he was motivated by the same influences that affected Chojun Miyagi and the latter's 'Hard/Soft Way'. After a while, Mabuni changed his mind about the name of his style and decided to call it Shito Ryu (pronounced 'Sh'toe-reeoo).

This name came about through a combination of the Japanese characters of his teachers' names.

Shito Ryu is one of the major styles of Karate in the world. Its katas are extremely beautiful, using high stances and long movements. It is no surprise to learn that some of the world's greatest kata exponents are from the Shito Ryu School. There are some quite marked similarities, as one might expect, between Goju Ryu and Shito Ryu though the movements in Shito Ryu are not quite so heavy and ponderous.

One of the offshoots from Shito Ryu in recent years, has come about through the work of the teacher Shigeru Kimura. Kimura is the student of Chojiro Tani, who in turn learnt from the founder of the Shito Ryu, Kenwa Mabuni. Tani, like all the other great teachers before him, developed a variant of his mother style which he named 'Taniha-Shitoryu'. This variant was further refined by Kimura and has become known nowadays as 'Shukokai' ('Way for All').

Shukokai

Shukokai is one of the most interesting forms of Karate and has undergone its development during recent times. Kimura was deeply concerned with the generation of power in Karate techniques and so he set about studying and researching ways of developing it. During his lectures, he made frequent mention of the use of a computer to substantiate his theories but was more convincing when he demonstrated them by means of an old inner tube!

Many karateka of other styles became interested in his studies and joined with him. At first, his basic, leaning forward stance opened competition minded Shukokai karateka to a wide range of counter attacks. As Shukokai became more established, however, its karateka learned to leave their basic style at the ringside, in order to concentrate on the totally singular activity that is known as sport karate.

The Shukokai system soon began to show real advances in striking power, the fist techniques being based upon a delivery from a stressed, upright stance, with the knees forced outward. The hip winds back before a punch is delivered, just as though a bow was being drawn taut. The hip is then released and rotates forward, bringing the punching arm following behind it. The punch is thus 'thrown' into the target in a more passive way than in other schools. Though one might imagine the double hip-twist slows the reaction time, in practice it does not do so significantly and Shukokai punches are the strongest to be found in Karate.

One of Kimura's senior students is Tommy Morris from Glasgow, Scotland. Morris is able to demonstrate quite convincingly how recoil is best soaked up by a moving body. He demonstrates the shortcomings of the traditional karate forward stance by advancing upon the outstretched punching arm and by applying direct pressure thereon (as would be, if the punch landed), he is able to show that the front foot of the punching karateka has a tendency to lift.

In place of this rigid method of attempting to control recoil, Morris explains how Shukokai encourages a forward body movement behind the punch; the momentum of the moving body effectively absorbing the impact recoil.

Similarly with the Shukokai kicks, the body moves behind the foot, raising, in the case of the front kick, up onto the ball of the supporting leg. Projecting the hips forward during the kick, means that extra power is thrown in behind the kicking leg and as an incidental bonus, the quickly rising knee and closed groin render a direct counter more difficult.

The Shukokai roundhouse kick is also curious by comparison with other schools in the way it depends upon an impact for stability. The karateka delivering the kick leans the upper body away and allows the hip of the kicking leg to rise up and over the hip of the supporting leg. The result of this is great power but less possibility of a safe withdrawal if the target becomes unreachable.

As a final point, no description of Shukokai is complete without reference to the punching pad used in the style. Many schools of Karate use a punching post, or 'Makiwara' but generally these are intended to condition the knuckles. Repeated use causes painful bruising and abrasion to them. The Shukokai punching pad is very much a child of the twentieth century, being made of layers of closed cell expanded plastic foam. When these are held against the chest, a karateka can land blow after blow on them without causing damage either to the attacker or to the person holding the pad.

Wado Ryu

The development of new styles continued and some sprang direct from Funakoshi's Shotokan. The latter cases were purely Japanese and based, to a greater or lesser extent, upon the teachings of Funakoshi himself. This means that they were largely divorced at the outset from the original Okinawa-te. One such style is Wado Ryu, the 'Way of Peace' which was devised by Funakoshi's student, Hironori Ohtsuka. Ohtsuka was a classical Japanese Budo man, with a good knowledge of Shindo Yoshin Ryu Jiu Jitsu. One of his actions was to change the names of his system's kata back to Chinese and thus Funakoshi's Heian katas became Ohtsuka's Pinans, Kanku became Ku Shanku and Gankaku, Chinto etc.

The Wado Ryu basic stance was higher than the Shotokan and the movements both faster and lighter. Ohtsuka sought the development of power through light movements which were snapped back from the extremity of their travel. The result of this was to create a whiplash effect. Ohtsuka also developed a system of prearranged sparring which he called 'Kihon Kumite'. This embodies the principles of Wado Ryu which are seen to be based upon evasion, or deflection. The use of lateral evasion to escape a blow contrasts sharply with the back and forth movement of Shotokan karateka.

It is also in these Kihon that a residue of Ohtsuka's classical Budo training is seen. In one of them, the punch is trapped and a wristlock/throw employed. The wristlock is a perfectly standard Jiu Jitsu or Aikido item, duplicated in both syllabuses. Such holds are not found within the Shotokan school.

Kyokushinkai

Another of Funakoshi's students was the Korean, Masutatsu Oyama. There is also a reference to his having trained in Goju Kai under Gogen Yamaguchi. Oyama is one of the more flamboyant Karate innovators. In his youth, he states that he was impressed by the Chinese wrestler, Lee San and learned various techniques from him.

After practising Shotokan for a time, Oyama founded his own school, which he called 'Kyokushinkai' – 'The Way of Ultimate Truth'. During the origination of this style, he spent eighteen months living like a hermit in the mountains. Unkind critics have claimed that the reasons for this isolation are based upon less esoteric grounds. Whatever the reasons, Oyama became concerned with a return to truly effective Karate and he scathingly described Funakoshi's Karate-do as mere exercises.

Despite the fact that Oyama sought a return to effective Karate, he evidently recognised the interest shown in competitions and accordingly developed a form more in keeping with his views. The name of this is 'Knockdown'. It allows full power strikes to the body and full power kicks to the body and head. The face is not a target area and as a result of this, it is not

A high stance is characteristic of Wado Ryu Karate

uncommon to see two tired fighters leaning on each other whilst pummelling away at the body.

The system also allows kicks to the thighs and legs, so whilst it is one of the less aesthetically pleasing forms of Karate competition, it is nevertheless, one of the toughest!

Modern Karate styles do not go in for a great deal of body conditioning and when taking part in a Knockdown competition students frequently learn this deficiency to their cost!

Like Ohtsuka, Oyama returned to using older Chinese titles for his katas such as the term 'Pinan' for the first five basic ones. The school also favours a curious circular block which is found only in Taekwondo. Kyokushinkai seems to be continually evolving and its founder is now looking outside Karate for new techniques and concepts to incorporate.

Shotokai

One of the saddest breaks for Funakoshi had he been alive came when his senior student, Egami, broke away to form the Shotokai. Egami represented the nucleus of the growing dissatisfaction within the Japan Karate Association over the way Karate development was going. Egami opposed large scale teaching and the changes this forced upon the system. Two of the karateka he took with him when he broke away were Tsutomo Oshima and Mitsusuke Harada. Oshima went to live in Los Angeles whilst Harada eventually arrived in London, being the first Japanese instructor to take up residence there.

The Shotokai of Oshima follows closely the present form of Shotokan though there are differences. Notably these are that the punching arm is not fully extended in the former school and there is a larger use of 'immovable stance'. The movements are also more fluid and less jerky than Shotokan. Harada's Shotokai has gone a great deal further and can only barely be compared with Shotokai taught by European teachers such as Hattori of Spain.

Karateka of more orthodox schools cannot understand or appreciate Harada's Shotokai. They have been raised on a diet of hard techniques and cannot comprehend how a seemingly soft block or punch can be effective. Presumably such karateka would also fail to understand anything of the so called 'soft' but effective systems of Kung Fu! People on the receiving end of a Shotokai punch report that it is extremely powerful. There is also a recorded instance of a mature Shotokai karateka sparring with a young Shotokan international Karate fighter. The latter didn't stand a chance, simply because the Shotokai man had obviously learned the concepts of distance and timing, both of which allowed him to move aside, or inside, as the younger man attacked.

The tragedy with Harada's Shotokai is that being far removed from physical principles, it is impossible to teach it. Harada can only teach by example, showing by means of incredible demonstrations how an apparently soft movement can bowl over a would-be attacker.

Shotokan

Shotokan, on the other hand, is very clearly presented and taught, as befits the style that originated from Funakoshi. It is worth noting that there was only one Karate-do, as far as he was concerned. It was a source of real disappointment to him that he was unable to unite all the styles of Karate under the banner of the JKA.

Much of the work on producing the modern Shotokan image came from Funakoshi's son, Yoshitake. The latter was responsible for lowering and extending the stances into the now familiar format of this particular school. Shotokan involves the use of great muscle effort. During the punch, muscle contraction is pronounced and this may readily be seen in the contorted faces of Shotokan karateka. Blocking movements are large, with every effort made to squeeze an extra amount of force out. By comparison, the kicks are somewhat disappointing.

The roundhouse kick uses mainly the ball of the foot and its wide swinging mode of delivery makes for easy early identification by the opponent. The side kick does not utilise an in-line thrust of the body and it is difficult to see the side snap kick as having any effect whatsoever upon the determined attacker.

The katas are well thought out and very numerous. The use of low stances, coupled with slow and deliberate movements, makes them rather attractive to watch. For many years the Shotokan kata experts were regarded as the best in the world but now their supremacy has been successfully challenged by the Shito Ryu and Shukokai.

Others

To be sure, there are many other styles of Karate practised in the world and some of them are what would be called 'family styles'. Others are fairly well spread and show interesting techniques, one such being the Yuishinkai school of Moto-kase Inoue. This school is devoted to the old Okinawan arts which included not only the unarmed but also the armed systems of attack and defence. The school is notable for teaching knife defence techniques as part of the syllabus. Its kicks tend to be aimed at targets below the waist – in much the same way that Funakoshi himself preferred. The Yuishinkai punch is curious in that the thumb is kept uppermost during delivery.

This particular fist is also used in the Isshin Ryu ('Of One Mind') school of Shimabuku. Isshin Ryu is a fairly recent school, having been developed in 1955 from a mixture of different Okinawan schools. Entirely coincidentally, another Ishin Ryu Karate Karate Association came into being in Britain. It has no connection with Shimabuku's school and its members are notable competitors in international sports karate tournaments. This latter Ishin Ryu has been founded by David 'Ticky' Donovan and it is a blending of Kyokushinkai with Wado Ryu and Shotokan.

Another exponent of the complete Okinawa-te is Teruo Hayashi. Hayashi has rekindled interest in the study of the Okinawan art both in Japan and Okinawa. He founded his school of Kenshin Ryu after studying the styles of Shito Ryu and Goju Ryu. As a result of Hayashi's initiative, Japanese and Okinawan Karateka are returning to a study of weaponry and there have been several exciting free fighting displays between appropriately armed karateka.

Karate was introduced to Europe by a Japanese instructor who did not practise one of the major styles. Hiroo Mochizuki came to Paris, on the invitation of Henri Plee in 1956 and taught the style of Yoseikan there. This style is named after the Dai Nihon Yoseikan Bujutsukai where the young Mochizuki was taught the classical Japanese arts. Yoseikan is a family style and has no relationship to the Karate introduced to Japan by Funakoshi. It has some similarities to Inoue's Yuishinkai and Shimabuku's Isshin Ryu; in particular, the thumb of the punching fist is uppermost.

Uechi Ryu is one of the more curious styles of Okinawan Karate, being named after the founder, Kanbun Uechi (pronounced 'Way-Chee'). Uechi trained in mainland China, under the direction of the Chinese Master Chou Tzu-Ho. There is some confusion over the style, or styles of Chinese martial art that he learned. Uechi claimed he trained in the 'Pangai Noon' style but no current experts on Chinese martial arts history have ever heard of it.

Pangai Noon was claimed to comprise Dragon, Tiger and Crane styles and an examination of Uechi Ryu certainly does show some of their characteristics.

The basic practice stance is the familiar sanchin stance. Students are urged to practise little else but this for a number of years – so as to develop the strength and stability needed to master the style. The arms are held in rather a peculiar way with the hands carried palms down, open and twisted to the outside. The whole effect is similar to the Dragon school of Kung Fu.

Students use the 'Phoenix Eye' one knuckle punch a great deal, and there is little evidence of that staple part of more common Karate, the hip twist. On the contrary, power is generated by spasmodic jerks of all the muscles in the manner of the hard Kung Fu schools. Kicks are characteristically low but unusually use the tips of the toes as the impact area! Naturally this technique takes a great deal of learning, conditioning and courage.

The appearance of yet another latter-day style indicates the continuing dense branching of the family tree of Karate. Sankukai is named after the Founder, Yoshinao Nanbu. Nanbu was born in 1943, into a family deeply interested in the martial arts. For a while he studied Shukokai with Chojiro Tani but eventually left to found Sankukai. Being of an inventive turn of mind, he originated a whole series of katas and defined the principles of Sankukai as being based upon circular motions. Being such a comparatively young man, it caused something of a stir in more conservative Karate circles when he promoted himself to 10th Dan! Not content with Sankukai, Nanbu has since developed another Karate system which he calls 'Nanbudo'.

This last example illustrates clearly the difficulties that are encountered when trying to trace Karate development. There have been so many splits and so many schools set up that it becomes very difficult to trace the linkages. It is not clear when to recognise one style whilst dismissing another. Did the teachers of Funakoshi decry his new Karate-do? It is certain that some did, calling it ineffectual and incomplete. Yet that school is now, after the passage of time, one of the respectable ones that new styles are measured against.

With time sometimes comes a measure of respectability. A master whose students go out and win major sport karate tournaments is sure to receive a more ready acceptance of his new style than someone who is not known and maybe even mis-spells the Japanese name of his new school! Now that Karate has reached so many countries and become so popular, the rate of break-up must logically increase, for there is no overall firm leadership. It is no longer important to claim a relationship with an 'authentic' Japanese association. What, after all, is an authentic Japanese association and for how long has it been considered authentic?

The stances of Karate
The techniques of Karate are delivered from a number of stances, each of which is suited for a particular purpose or situation. The most elementary stance to start with has the body upright, with the palms of the hands resting against the front of the thighs. The posture is erect, the legs are straight, with the heels touching and the feet slightly splayed. This

stance leads to a more advanced state of readiness, produced by clenching the fists and stepping to the side, first with the left foot, then with the right foot.

When adopting this latter stance, it is important not to separate the feet too widely. Their outside edges should lie on a vertical line dropping from the shoulders to the ground. The knees may be very slightly bent and the stomach muscles relaxed. From this stance, any of the following stances may be formed.

Step forward a pace with the left leg and straighten the rear right leg. The front leg is now bent so that its knee lies above the middle of the foot. It is important to ensure this relationship since it is all too easy to put weight onto the outer edge of the foot, causing a bowlegged appearance. The knee of the rear leg must be locked straight.

When stepping forward, do make sure that the width of the ready stance is retained. Don't let the moving left foot come diagonally inwards. The object is to get a stance which is both stable in a fore and aft direction and in addition, has a lateral stability produced by not having the feet in the same line. The hips must be directed fully forward and not angled back in any way. If this is properly done, there will be a need to stop the rear leg from bending slightly and the rear foot will face three-quarters forward. Hold the fists loosely to the sides of the body.

When stepping forward into the opposite stance, make sure that there is no bobbing up and down, by keeping the supporting legs bent. Holding the fists to the sides, step forward and ensure that the new rear leg locks straight behind and side-step has been maintained, i.e. the heels haven't come into line.

From the forward stance, try a simple turn and to do this, bend the rear leg and slide it across and behind the front. The rear leg should move an equal distance to the other side of the front foot. Make sure, though, that the step is made across only and don't bring the leg forward to meet the front one. Rest the rear foot on its ball and keep the knee bent. Starting with the hips, rotate the lower body and allow the shoulders to follow behind. As the body rotates, let more and more weight come on the previously rear foot. At the completion of the turn, the rear foot has become the front foot of a new forward stance facing in the reverse direction. Remember that once the rear leg has been placed in preparation for the turn, the feet only swivel; there are no further steps.

The forward stance practised between turns is the platform for delivering a basic punch and in some schools it is also used to kick from. The exact length of forward stance will vary. In Shotokan, it is extremely low and long. Shotokan karateka feel that its length gives them great stability when under attack and provides a firm foundation for punches. A long forward stance also has the advantage of strengthening the upper leg muscles.

From forward stance, rotate the hips slightly more forward, turning the front foot inwards and drawing it back, to make the stance a little shorter. The feet should now be parallel, or slightly converging. This stance is used for the delivery of a very important technique called 'Reverse Punch'.

To step from one reverse punch stance to another is not a straightforward process. To begin with, the leading foot must be rotated outwards and only then is the rear leg brought up to it and then swept forwards and outwards in a shallow 'u'. Whilst drawing the leg forward, it is important to keep both bent so that the height of the stance doesn't change. As the

Reverse punch is a much used Karate technique

Forward stance is the basic position for delivering lunge punch

new leading foot takes up its position, the opposite hip begins to rotate fully forward, causing the rear foot also to swivel. It is this important hip action which acts as the powerhouse of the reverse punch. The turn from reverse punch stance is exactly the same as that used for the forward stance.

By keeping the feet converging and drawing back the front foot still further, a stage is reached where if both knees are bent, they will actually touch one another. When this stage is reached, the stance is of the correct length for sanchin. Tense up all of the muscles and force the hips forward. Rotate the knees outwards but keep the feet converging. This will cause all of the body weight to be taken on the outside edges of the feet. Remember to clench the fists tightly and do not relax for the duration of the stance.

A far more relaxed stance is obtained when the feet are both turned forwards and the leading foot drawn back so that its heel is just in front of the toes of the rear foot. The rear foot is rotated slightly outwards and will take much of the weight of

Left: Cat stance has all the weight on the back foot. It is useful for kicking with the front leg

Right: Back stance is not as extreme as cat stance. Here, the weight distribution is 75/25 per cent in favour of the back foot

the body. This is a useful stance for delivering a sudden attack, sliding forwards on the front foot and driving off the rear to produce a quick forward movement. As in the case of all the previous stances, the turn is performed by merely stepping across with the rear leg and using the hips.

Next, slide the front foot forward a little further than in the previous stance. Keep the entire weight over the rear foot by bending and keeping it directly under the backside.

The foot that slides forward actually points straight ahead, whilst the rear foot remains slightly turned out. The heel of the front foot can be raised from the floor, so that only the ball is in contact. This stance is known as the 'Cat Stance'. It is very useful for fast snap kicks off the front leg. Because the heels are in line, the stance is not very stable in a lateral direction.

From cat stance, continue to slide the forward foot whilst keeping the weight as much as possible on the rear leg. To accommodate the increased stretch, the supporting leg can swivel further and this means that the body will turn side-on,

Horse riding or straddle stance uses an equal weight distribution. It is useful for strengthening the legs and as a launch position for side kick

whereas previously it was front facing. This new position is known as the 'Back Stance'. Depending upon the particular school, the fore foot may either lie flat on the ground, or the heel may be raised slightly — as in cat stance.

There are two varieties of side stance, the one involving the feet rotated outwards and the other with them parallel, or slightly converging. The first type is similar to that used by sumo wrestlers. The body is suspended midway between the bent legs and the back is held straight with the hips pushed forwards. It is important not to push the backside out! When bending the legs, keep the knees always above the ankles and don't let them drop inwards. To achieve this, keep the knees rotated outwards, as in sanchin stance.

The second variety of side stance is similar to the above except in respect of the feet. This side stance is much more difficult to maintain than the previous one.

'Fighting Stance' is the name given to a posture that is used extensively in free sparring. The stance is of medium length — not too short and not too long. The feet are parallel, with the

Fighting stance is a flexible posture from which many different moves may be made

front foot turned in slightly to guard the groin. Both knees are slightly bent. The fore-hand is held as a fist, level with the height of the shoulder. The elbow is bent approximately ninety degrees. The rear fist is held ready and palm up in the region of the knot in the belt. It is important to keep both elbows in and not to flap them during movement.

During the practice of Karate, a stance may be maintained for only a fraction of a second but in that time the posture must be correct if the technique is to be effective.

The weapons of Karate

Virtually every part of the body is used as a weapon in Karate. The most popular idea of the Karate technique is the so called 'Karate Chop', otherwise known as 'Knife Hand'. Surprisingly, this technique is less often used than might be imagined. The most used hand weapon in the karateka's armoury is the front fist. This is formed by rolling the fingers into the palm of the hand, touching them against the little fleshy pad that runs along their base. If the fist is properly made, there will be a right angle between the fingers and the back of the hand. This right angle is important and the fist must be made and remade until it is obtained. Without it, the lower joints of the fingers will strike the target ahead of the knuckles, causing injury.

A good way to develop the correct angle is to make a fist and then lean on it against a table top. To complete the correctly formed front fist, lock the thumb down and around the first two fingers. Never make a fist with the thumb tucked inside since this can cause a dislocation. Never allow the thumb to project out where it can get hooked up in sleeves and suchlike.

The front fist uses only the two larger knuckles of the index and middle finger to deliver its impact. The reason for this is the smaller the area of contact that force is delivered over, the greater the effect of that force. Try this by first pressing on the chest with the flat of the palm and then applying the same pressure but using the middle joint of the thumb to transmit it. The latter is more painful.

Front fist is also generally delivered with the palm facing downwards. An exception to this occurs in one school which demonstrates quite reasonably that punching upwards with the palm down means that the lower knuckles again make first (and painful!) contact with the target. Their remedy is to rotate the fist thumb uppermost when striking a high target and gradually rotating it into the more orthodox palm down for-

The impact areas are shaded

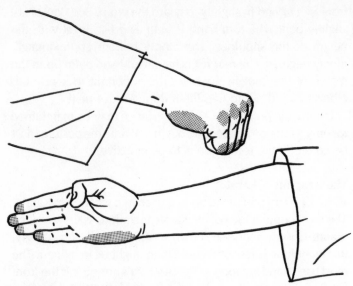

mat, when punching a low target.

Front fist may also be used as an effective club; the clenched fingers raising a line of muscle along the little finger side. This part of the fist is quite useful for blocking a technique. The 'Hammerfist', as it is called, is swung into the target rather like a baton. This punch is one of the safer ones to use, since muscle cushions the impact area and there is no chance of bruising bone – unless the wrist accidentally hits something hard.

By using a loose wrist action, the front fist can also be used to snap strike to the side of the opponent's face. To do this, the back of the large two knuckles is used. The fist is swung as an arc, stopping just short of the target. The loose wrist then allows the back fist to hinge forward with a snapping motion.

Unfolding the fingers halfway allows the middle joints to be used as a weapon against soft targets, such as the opponent's stomach. Remember to keep the thumb bent in and held rigid, so there's little chance of it getting caught. If the half open fist is then bent back on the wrist, the palm heel can be used to great effect on such targets as the chin. This weapon is excellent for those people with weak wrists, or those who cannot pull their fingers back into a proper ninety degree fist. Palm heel is found in other martial arts and in Kung Fu, the fingers sometimes completely open out – something that is not seen in Karate.

Keeping with the palm heel, open the fingers a little, leaving them in a hooked shape. Let the thumb also move away from its customary locked-in safety position. This is the claw hand, a particularly vicious weapon when used against the face. The hooked fingers easily catch in the eyes, with the possibility of very severe injury. This weapon should be used with great care!

The claw hand is also used to grab the opponent's shoulder or sleeve as in Goju Ryu Karate. Certain styles of Kung Fu also use claw hand and plunge the hands repeatedly into sand, cinders, or small stones, so as to harden the tips of the fingers.

From the claw hand, extend the fingers out fully and lock in the thumb across the palm. This allows four areas of the hand to be used. The first and best known is the knife hand, using the pad of flesh lying from near the base of the little finger to just above the wrist. The knife hand is frequently used as a block by sweeping it palm out and with the fingers pointing upwards, across the face, with the little finger side preceding. It can also be used as a weapon, against the collar-bone, the neck, or the groin. During delivery, the hand may be slightly cupped and the angle of attack will depend upon the target.

The thumb side of the knife hand may also be used but remember to move the thumb as far inwards as it will go. The impact area of this less used weapon is the base of the index finger. To deliver ridge hand, as it is called, the hand moves palm down in an arc, using a bent elbow during delivery. Typical targets would be the front of the face, the throat, or the temples.

The tips of the fingers form a fearsome weapon named 'Spearhand' but the proper use of this requires a good degree of hand conditioning. Some teachers will bend the middle finger, so as to bring its tip into line with the index and fourth fingers. The striking area so formed is trained by thrusting it first into a soft medium such as flour, then moving through to sand and finally to pebbles, or twists of bamboo slivers. After such prolonged training, the hand becomes veritably like a spear! It is important to note that whilst a trained instructor can break wood with the spearhand, anyone else is sure to end up with a dislocation if they try.

The spearhand figured large in the training of the Okinawan masters but its use has largely died out now in the modern schools of Karate. The reason for this is the degree of hand conditioning required. From the past come tales of how the spearhand could be driven into the body of the opponent, whereupon it would close around the viscera, dragging them forth with the withdrawal! This horrific technique is enacted in one of the karate katas, though the understanding of the

The double finger strike is used to attack the eyes

move has, in many cases, been lost.

The final use of the extended hand is a technique rather like back fist, in that the two large knuckles and back of the fist proper are used against the side of the opponent's jaw, in a type of back-handed slap. This part of the hand is also useful as a block guiding an incoming punch out to the side of the face. When used in this manner, the wrist is bent outwards slightly, so as to reduce the chance of the fist brushing over its top and continuing on to strike the face.

Sometimes a single finger is used to poke at the eyes, or groin. In this case, the index finger of a normal front fist is straightened. When attacking the eyes, the middle finger may also straighten, making a two-pronged weapon. Yet another weapon used against the soft areas of the opponent is the One Knuckle Punch, a technique found throughout all the unarmed systems. It is most prevalent in certain styles of Kung Fu, where it is known as Phoenix Eye Punch. To form the weapon, make a normal forefist, then slightly push forward the middle finger, so that its middle joint comes to point forwards. To hold it in position, close the index and fourth fingers in behind its lower joint and hold them across with the thumb. The impact area is that solitary middle joint.

The final hand weapon to be mentioned is the back of the wrist itself. This is most commonly used as a block; the hand being bent forwards and the elbow low. In use, it knocks the incoming technique upwards and a curious, little used follow-through may then be used. During the formation of this block the thumb and all the fingers touch at their tips, making a beak-like shape. This weapon can be used to attack the eyes

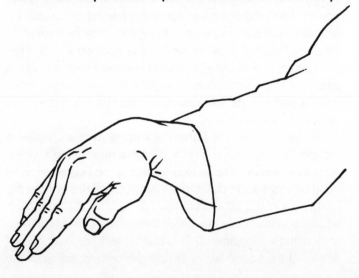

The upper surface of the wrist is used as a blocking area

A horizontal elbow strike is a very effective short-range move

following the wrist block. It is widely found in Kung Fu and is a main weapon of the White Crane School, where it is used to simulate a beak pecking.

It is curious that there has been an overall move away from finesse when using the weapons of Karate. The majority of them are used as hammers, to smash the opponent by means of a great deal of power developed by specialised stances and scientific application of momentum and recoil. It is interesting to speculate why greater heed was not paid to striking at the opponent's weak points. The use of such weak points means that techniques have to be less forceful; though, on the other hand, they do have to be placed with a greater degree of accuracy if they are to have an effect. It is said that, even as the lines on the palms of the hands differ, so the exact location of certain of the weak points may vary from person to person.

When using the elbow as a weapon, it is important to maximise force over the smallest possible impact area – as was done with the front fist – using only the point of the elbow to deliver the impact. It is important to avoid striking the funny-bone and this can be avoided by rotating the fist prior to delivery.

The elbow can be used in a variety of ways. With someone standing behind, take a short step back and turn the hip. As the weight settles down on the rear leg, bring the elbow directly back. It is important, when delivering the technique, to ensure that the elbow strike is delivered just as the hip twists and the weight comes back down on the rear leg. To increase the force of the blow, the elbow can be given extra room in which to accelerate by first extending the striking arm and opening out the fingers, as though to shake hands with someone. As the elbow is about to make contact, the open hand is suddenly pulled into a fist and the spasm of this gives an extra bonus in impact.

The elbow can also be used to attack the chin of a taller person. Imagine standing close to an opponent. Take a half step forwards with the left leg and bring the right arm, which is bent ninety degrees at the elbow, in an upward arc, so that the elbow strikes just under the chin. Extra power is gained here by allowing the hips to rotate behind the elbow and by slightly straightening the bent legs at the moment of impact.

A third way to use the elbow is in the form of a horizontal

The elbow is used in several different ways. On the left the exponent uses a back elbow to someone standing behind him. On the right a descending elbow strike is used

arc – like the forearm smashes of Saturday afternoon TV wrestlers.

Commence with the left leg forwards for example and in this case, use the right elbow. When using this technique, the hips must move freely, allowing the bent elbow to travel into its target – which may be the side of the face, or the base of the opponent's sternum.

Moving now to feet techniques, virtually all parts of the feet can be used as weapons. To begin, rest the foot flat on the floor and then raise the heel off as far as possible so that only the ball of the front is touching the floor. Try to get the instep all in one line with the shin. This configuration is precisely what is needed to form the foot ready for front kick. It is important to keep that instep extended because any hingeing at the ankle will not only weaken the kick but will also result in the possibility of ankle injury. It is also important to make sure that the toes are pulled back out of harm's way when using the front kick. They are easily dislocated or fractured!

The upward travelling elbow is particularly useful from close range

The impact areas are shaded

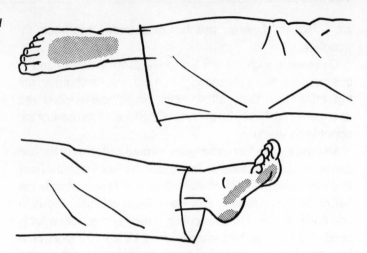

The ball of the foot may also be used in a short range roundhouse kick, where the foot travels in a horizontal arc.

The instep is a useful weapon to use against the groin, side of the face, or the floating ribs. Care must be taken when using it, since contact with the opponent's elbow (very easy when kicking at the floating ribs) is extremely painful. The safest and most effective target for the instep is undoubtedly the groin. A direct groin kick is useful if facing the attacker. If at a slight angle, then the kick must be given a corresponding slight turn-in to get past the thigh.

In both cases, the kick must be snapped out, rather like cracking a whip. The upper leg muscles power the kick,

For side kick, stand in side straddle stance

Maintain guard and lift forward leg. Knee is bent

Thrust out the kicking leg whilst swivelling on the supporting foot. Strike with the heel

After execution retrieve kick promptly

A

B

allowing the knee to rise until it is pointed at the opponent's groin. At this stage, the upper leg is braked to a sudden stop and the loose knee joint allows the lower leg to travel on passively. As the instep contacts the target, the upper leg swings back, 'snapping' the kick back and preventing it from being caught in the event that the strike was unsuccessful.

The best stance from which to use the groin kick is the cat stance. The forward leg is resting only lightly on the floor and requires the smallest effort to use it quickly. Since the groin is such a sensitive area, no great power is needed to achieve results. Do make sure though, when using this kick, that the toes are fully extended and the upper surface of the foot curved slightly downwards.

The heel is also a very good weapon to use in various ways. The most common is the side kick and this may be practised from one of the straddle stances, or from the fist clenched, ready stance. Begin by leaning away from the attacker and raising the knee of the leg closest to him. The lean away is useful in that it takes the face away from attack and means that the opponent must lean forwards to reach – a very unstable position to be in. When the upper leg is more or less horizontal, drive the heel out and down, aiming at the opponent's kneecap. To generate additional power, the supporting leg should be slightly bent and as the kick begins, that leg drags in the same direction. Only a short drag is necessary to bring body weight behind the impact. At the same time as the

C   D

For back kick, from back stance, step across with the front foot

Put weight on the front foot and swivel so that your back is towards the target

A

B

foot drags, rotate it away from the kick's direction. The effect of this latter move will be to extend the kick by opening the hips.

The correct foot alignment is a little difficult to achieve at first. The first stage pulls the foot into a right angle to the shin. The second stage involves lifting the big toe and depressing the others, so that an edge is given to the foot. If one toe cannot be raised independently of the others, then merely raise or depress all of the toes to achieve a nearly comparable effect. Whichever is achieved, make sure that when the kicking leg is extended, the heel is furthest out and first actually to contact the opponent.

The back kick is slightly simpler and to get the foot right, just lift the instep as far as possible, leaving the heel projecting. Start the kick from a fighting or a forward stance and keep the elbows close to the body during delivery. Look over the shoulder to get a fix on the target and pick up the front foot. Drive it out backwards like a pistol whilst leaning forwards to counter the weight of the extended foot. Keep the head up, otherwise balance will be lost. This kick is aimed at the opponent's groin when he is standing behind.

C   D

Finally, use the heel to attack a fallen opponent by bringing it up as high as possible on a straight leg and then letting it fall, like an axe, onto his head or stomach. Form the foot exactly as for the back kick.

Drive out the kicking leg like a piston with the heel forward. Do not look over your shoulder

The inside edge of the kick is sometimes used in a wiping motion across the opponent's body. The foot is held normally but the sole is curled inwards, so as to make a scoop. The toes point vertically in the air as the foot travels in a flat arc across the opponent's guard, knocking his front arm across or down and creating an opening for a decisive attack. The inner edge can also be used to scoop up an opponent's foot — especially if he was just about to step forward onto it. When the opponent's leg is taken with such a leg sweep, it must be taken the way it is pointing; only in this way can a lighter person sweep a heavier. When executing the sweep, make sure that the body leans back and the face is guarded. The opponent may just lash out in desperation as he feels his balance going!

Withdraw the kicking leg and place it down lightly then swivel around to face forwards

The knee is a strong weapon but, like the elbow, it is of use only during a close-up situation. Simply grab the opponent's hair with one hand, or link both behind his neck and pull his head down into the path of an upwards travelling knee. Alternatively, if the attacker is taller, drive the knee into the groin.

A variant of the knee attack is to use it in the form of an upward moving arc, so it travels part horizontally and part vertically. This 'Roundhouse Kneekick' is particularly effective if at an angle to the opponent and where a direct kneekick would only hit his thigh or arm. When using a roundhouse kneekick however, ensure that the supporting foot swivels in the direction of the strike in order to develop full power.

In conclusion, a few general comments are in order. The kick is generally more powerful than the punch, because the legs and their musculature are larger and heavier. On the other hand, because of their greater mass, they tend to be slower than the hands. Except for the knee, they are all middle to long distance techniques. There is no point in kicking someone in punching range because the punch will beat the kick at such close quarters.

When using a kick, use it as quickly as possible and always select a suitable target. In a real situation, do not kick above the groin – just as it is not wise to punch someone in the kneecap!

Blocks and evasions in Karate

It is not only important to be able to punch and kick but it is equally important to be able to prevent someone's attack from landing effectively. To achieve this, there are a number of blocks and evasions that can be used. The first is, quite simply, distance. If at a correct distance an attacker will not be able to

Using knife block the blocking arm is palm forwards and vertical

The blocking arm falls and extends forwards, the other extends back over the shoulder

The extended arm is pulled back violently and the other arcs around, coming to rest with the palm forward

Use knife block to stop a
punch attack to the face

reach the defender except by a step, or a pronounced lean.

Distance is a critical factor to consider when working with an opponent. Too great a distance means that neither can get anywhere near the other with a technique. If a stand-off situation is what is called for then standing too far away and maintaining that distance will achieve it. On the other hand, stand too close and the first one to strike may very well be the one that wins the fight.

The simplest way of dealing with an incoming technique is not to be there when it arrives! This is extremely important when dealing with an opponent who is much larger. In such cases, there could always be the possibility that an attempt to block will be unceremoniously swept aside. Most techniques are, after all, aimed at a target; if that target is moved even a little distance the right way, then the technique misses. Therefore, if someone throws a straight technique, step to either side and it will rattle on past.

When moving to the side, it is always advisable to step to what is called the 'closed' side. In a left fighting stance, for example, the closed side is on the left side of the body.

If the attacking technique is not a straight kick or punch but is rather a circular attack – such as a roundhouse kick – then either step back a little, or step in. The roundhouse kick is not quite as dangerous as it appears, since all the force of, say a turning kick, is generated at the extremity of the limb, i.e. the foot. If the defender moves inside the kick by sliding forwards a good way on the front leg, he will be placed in a position where the attacker has little chance of harming him. People are not too good at doing two things at once and the person who is concentrating on his roundhouse kick is not really in a good position – standing on one leg as he is – to deal with someone who has rather annoyingly moved in close.

It is possible also to step back, or even lean back a little. In this case, the circular technique passes harmlessly through the air in front. As the technique is about to miss, then that is the precise time to move in and counter. The attacker will not have recovered his technique and will be found to be vulnerable. However, take care because once his foot touches the ground, he will remember his combination technique and use a follow-up!

If faced with the necessity to block, then the defender must make sure he uses the minimum energy necessary to accomplish a deflection. There should be no attempt to meet might with might, because he might be stronger! Try stopping the shin of a fully powered front kick with the forearm and the latter will fracture. When blocking, always seek to deflect, to

Begin head block from a relaxed stance

Bring both arms forward and in front of the face in an 'X' configuration

Pull back one arm and use this to power the other upward and forward punch. Note the bent elbow

The head block deflects a punch to the face using the softer part of the forearm to cushion the impact

redirect the opponent's energy, so that he loses his balance and becomes prey for a counter.

To see the application of this, a head block can first be considered. Imagine that someone with a club is stepping up and swinging it downwards at the head. Step forwards so as to counter at a point where maximum force is not being generated. Block with the same side arm as the leg which is forwards. Punch across the face and towards the attacker. In this way, the blocking arm will intercept the descending blow at a very early point and provide a guide for it to slither harmlessly down the arm and past the shoulder. The harder the attacker strikes, the more likely he is to become unbalanced by the redirected force. Do note though, that to block the blow successfully, the elbow must be at the same level as the top of the head – otherwise the sliding and deflected club will hit the protruding part! Finally, be sure to rotate the blocking arm little finger upwards, so that the softer, lower surface of the arm is presented, cushioning the bones.

A mid section block can be performed moving back slightly from a forward, or fighting stance, into a back stance. At the same time, the leading hand can virtually slap an incoming punch to the side whilst leaving the defender close enough to counter-attack swiftly. To add fire to the block, the hand can turn inwards, palm towards the face, so that the punch is rapped rather sharply and painfully with the edge of a knife hand.

To evade front kick when in same stance as attacker, step to the side with the front foot, then swivel the hips. Scoop the kick up and forwards

Some styles of Karate advise blocking a great way from the body, whilst others suggest blocking close in. When deciding to block a good way from the body, the defender allows a greater margin of error, whereas if the block is in close, there is only a limited distance in which to stop the incoming technique. On the other hand, blocking a punch, by striking the attacking wrist will achieve a greater deflection for the amount of force used.

If an arm is held out straight and attempts made to deflect it by pushing to the elbow, they can be resisted. If, on the other hand the pressure is applied to the wrist, the rigid arm is easily moved. This is the principle of leverage.

Wherever possible, always use a block in conjunction with a body movement so as to be out of harm's way if the block itself fails. The block can be regarded as added insurance.

In the case of a straight kick, step out to the side with the front foot whilst swivelling the hips. Allow the feet to rotate and turn the body, by means of hip action, so as to turn into almost the same direction as the incoming kick. At the same time, use the front arm in a scooping motion to lift and deflect the kick. Incidentally, this particular move only works if both begin with the same leg forwards. If opposite legs are forward, then step out and back with the rear leg, transferring weight onto it and leaning away from the kick. Remember to draw up

Swivel the hips back and deliver a punch

the trailing rear leg and the kick will land somewhere behind the heels.

If confused with the concept of a different block for each different stance, then use distance to move back from, or into, the developing kick. If moving on to it though, keep the forward arm across the front like a bar. In this way, the opponent's shin is prevented from striking the groin. When moving in, extend the other arm in a punch.

The more skilled the student becomes, the less movement and effort is needed to block. There is absolutely no need to cross the hands over, so as to get a 'pull through' effect; neither is there any point in making large preparatory movements, because in a real situation, the incoming technique is travelling too fast to allow for them.

Developing power in Karate

The development of power in technique delivery is one of the main objectives in Karate. The Karate punch, for example, makes use of basic physics in its delivery from a stable stance. The first rule of basic physics to consider is the well-known equation that force equals mass times the square of the velocity that mass is travelling at. It will be recalled that such force as may be generated is delivered over the smallest area possible, so as to maximize impact.

Alternatively, to evade front kick, slide diagonally back from the kick

Having succeeded in blocking the kick, slide back into range, swivel the hips and punch. (This is to be used when in opposite stance to the attacker)

What the equation means is that a large person, punching slowly, may well generate a fair degree of force, whereas a lighter person must punch a very great deal faster in order to develop the same degree. A fast punch is, of course, a good thing to have, since it is less easy to intercept.

The Karate front punch uses a number of other devices to increase its effectivity. One of these is the rotating of the punch just prior to impact. Through most of its journey into the target, the punch will be travelling palm upwards and it is only as the target is reached, that the fist rotates sharply palm down and 'screws' in. This rotation of the fist is much used by boxers because it tears the skin over the target area.

Another device is the sudden exhaling of air in a grunt, or shout, just prior to impact. It is important, when doing this, to force the air from the diaphragm and at the same time, tighten up all the muscles. The effect of this sudden spasm and attendant shout, or grunt, is to inject a little more power into the blow.

When punching, the karateka always makes sure that the body is moving behind the blow. This is important since recoil can cause a light person literally to bounce off a heavier opponent. Momentum is gained by a moving body and even quite light people can generate considerable additional temporary mass by moving forwards in the wake of a strike.

All Karate punches use the hip, rather than the shoulder. In some punches, such as the front and reverse punch, the hip movement precedes the actual punch and travels in the same direction as it. The effect of this is to 'wind up' the spine, rather like an elastic band under torsion. When the spine 'unwinds'

For lunge punch begin from forward stance

Maintaining the forward fist, step forwards. Take care not to bob up and down

Settle onto the new front foot. Simultaneously lock the back leg straight, pull back the leading fist and drive out the punch. Note how the wrists twist in the last instant

For reverse punch start with parallel feet and punching hip facing forwards

Maintain the forward fist and slide the near leg forwards in a shallow 'U'

Simultaneously twist the hip forwards, withdraw the extended arm and punch

the shoulders follow the hips and the punch is sent on its way.

It is also common practice to withdraw the non-punching arm with the same degree of force that the punching arm is being extended. This concurrent movement throws the shoulder very violently behind the punch. Be careful though, when withdrawing the non-punching arm not to pull it back too far thus simultaneously opening the body to counter attack and removing the option of using a quick follow-up punch if the first misses.

In a punch such as the backfist, the hip actually rotates away from the strike, thus unrolling the bent striking arm into the target. This opening of the hips gives the strike a greater range but it is at the expense of sheer power.

Earlier in the Karate section, reference was made to Tommy Morris, the Shukokai karateka from Glasgow. Tommy emphasises the need to put weight on the front leg during punch delivery and shows how bending the front knee over its foot produces greater stability and penetration of the punch. He also stresses the need for the punching arm to be almost straight as it lands upon the target and uses the analogy of the billiard cue. If someone is poked with a cue it is painful, but if the cue is broken or hinged (i.e. the arm is bent at the elbow), the energy is sapped.

Meiji Suzuki also contributes a useful piece of information about the Karate punch. He advises those punching to the mid section of the opponent to strike downwards. The reason for this is that a powerful horizontal punch can knock someone backwards – their recoil reducing the effectiveness of the blow. If the punch is angled slightly downwards, however, the force is not applied horizontally, as in the first case and the opponent is knocked downwards onto the prop of his own rear leg.

Kicks also tend to rely greatly upon the hips and in the front

For front kick begin from fighting stance

Lift the kicking leg high whilst maintaining guard

Drive forward the kicking leg with toes pulled back. Note how the guard changes at this point

Snap back the kicking leg

Land gently on the kicking foot

For turning kick begin from fighting stance

Swivel hips and raise knee up and to side

Snap out the foot in a horizontal arc. Note that the toes are extended

Withdraw the leg prior to landing

A

B

C

D

kick, the supporting foot may swivel away from the direction in which the kick is travelling, so as to allow a full extension. A slight drag forward on the supporting leg does much to increase power.

During all kicks it is necessary to maintain an effective guard and a high kicking knee will serve to fend off an impetuous attacker. This trick is especially important in the case of a roundhouse kick where the initial movements must not be readily identifiable. Remember to lean the upper body away from counters and swivel on that supporting leg in order to bring the hip in behind the kick whilst at the same time ensuring maximum range.

Use the shout, or a grunt during the kick, just as for a punch or strike. This will ensure that maximum energy is put into the movement. Another advantage is that when the muscles of the stomach are contracted, the body is more able to take a blow. To try this, hold a lung full of air. As a blow lands, breathe out suddenly and lock the muscles tight in a spasm. The amount of impact that can be absorbed by this means is quite surprising. This is part of body conditioning and students are advised to include it on the training schedule.

Some schools encourage students to shout as they tense up. This is known as Kiai. Practising it in class reduces self-consciousness, but it is generally done wrongly – the student considering that the louder the shout, the more effective it is. Not only this but continuous kiai can be extremely wearing on the shouter's throat and equally wearing on the teacher's eardrums and the patience of those in the premises next door. Kiai performed properly, from the diaphragm, does not strain the throat.

Karate Training

Karate uses a ladder of progression to measure performance in the training hall. This ladder is identified by different coloured belts and the stages that relate to each belt are called the 'Kyu' grades. There are many different belt colour systems and a differing number of kyu grades leading to the coveted black belt. A typical school may have six or eight kyu grades and one colour scheme would be:–

Beginner	White Belt
8th Kyu	White Belt
7th Kyu	Yellow Belt
6th Kyu	Orange Belt
5th Kyu	Green Belt
4th Kyu	Purple Belt
3rd Kyu ⎱	
2nd Kyu ⎰	Brown Belt
1st Kyu	

The average interval between gradings varies from system to system with the interval increasing as the rank increases. Only a few months separate grades such as 7th and 8th kyu while at least a year would pass between 1st and 2nd dan.

In many ways, the institution of the coloured belt system has been a bad thing for Karate. Kyu grades often become preoccupied with the need to have visual evidence of advancement, to the detriment of their in-depth study of the art. The attitude in many cases is to race through the kyu grades to the black belt first dan. This is a suitable time to begin learning the art proper, since black belts only really mean that one has acquired a fair degree of skill in doing the mechanical movements and now the mind can be freed to concentrate on other things.

However, once students reach the black belt first dan, they see that in two years they can take the second dan examination and only three years after that, the third dan. The process continues except that it is not usual to take grades above third dan by means of a grading examination. In these higher grades, the pressures to pass examinations finally ease and only then may the black belt actually stop to reflect upon the nature of the martial art he has attained such a skill in.

Because some people do not progress as quickly through their grades as others, it is possible to reach the situation where someone who joined the club at a later stage holds a higher grade than perhaps a founding member. When this happens, the senior in time remains the class senior in the respect accorded, though usually the higher grade of the two will teach the class.

The one constant factor in the Karate dojo is respect. This respect is shown to the teacher by the students performing a formal bow. At the beginning and end of all training, the students perform a kneeling bow and each time they enter or leave the dojo (with the teacher's permission), they perform a standing bow. Even when the dojo is empty, it is customary to bow before entering or leaving it. In all cases, the bow is not obsequious, it is a measure of respect — the eyes are always looking forwards and never down at the floor.

Talking between the kyu grades is not permitted and the only sound to be heard in the well run traditional dojo is the breathing of the students as they train. Some dojos use a form of oath, which states the principles of Karate. Still others have a period of meditation whilst in a formal kneeling position. This is done with eyes closed and it is called 'Mokuso'. The idea behind mokuso is to encourage the development of a calm mind.

The practice of Karate, in whatever form, produces a kind of concentration which is relaxing in the extreme. Normal daytime worries vanish during the performance of the strenuous practice, so that Karate has come to be known as 'Moving Zen'.

Karate training is roughly the same in all schools, consisting of exercises (often inexpertly selected and practised), followed by basic technique. The latter is performed in lines and sometimes, these lines are graduated according to the level of skill of the karateka. Basic technique takes the form of repetitions of basic punches and/or kicks. When the heads of the lines begin to run out of training space, the order to turn is given and the group proceeds in the opposite direction. Regard basic technique as learning the alphabet of Karate.

After basic technique there is combination technique. This, as its name implies, combines basic punches and kicks together into a continuous movement. Some of the sequences are quite complex and may involve one or more stance changes. This form of training is an important part of Karate and teaches students how to move quickly from one technique to another.

Low grade karateka sparring always tend to use a single attack – pause – then a single attack again. This is because they have not yet mastered the flowing interplay of punches and kicks that are the basis of combination technique. Combination technique can be regarded as the building up of simple words from the alphabet of the basic techniques.

Kata

From simple groups of techniques the class moves to what is called 'kata'. This is a form of defence against multiple imaginary assailants. When there was no sparring in Karate, the kata was used as the highest form of practice. There are many sorts of kata, from simple training sequences designed to teach a particular stance or technique, to fully fledged systems of great complexity. An example of the former type would be the elementary katas, termed Pinans, or Heians, depending upon the style practised. An example of the latter type is 'Kanku Dai,' or 'Ku Shanku', this being one of the longest and most involved.

Some katas are based upon old Okinawan forms, whilst others are recently devised to be used as teaching aids. The older katas are interesting in that they contain moves for which no logical explanation can be found. One of the reasons given for this is that they were introduced into the kata so as to disguise its original intent from prying eyes.

The Wado Ryu Kata 'Pinan Nidan'

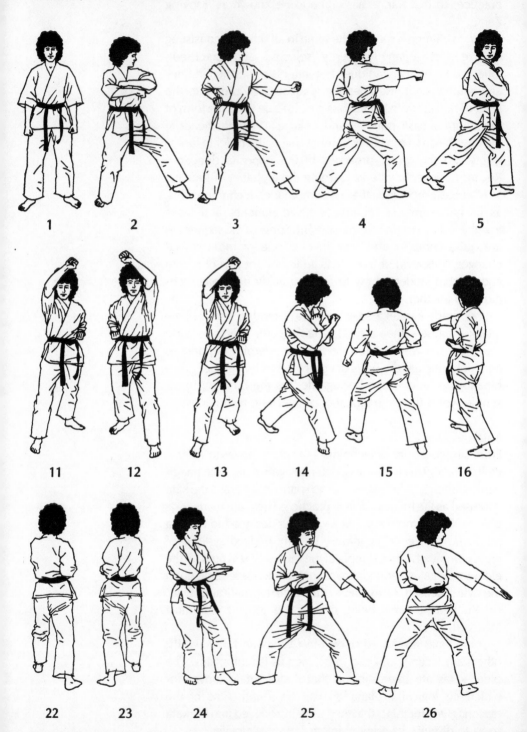

1   2   3   4   5

11   12   13   14   15   16

22   23   24   25   26

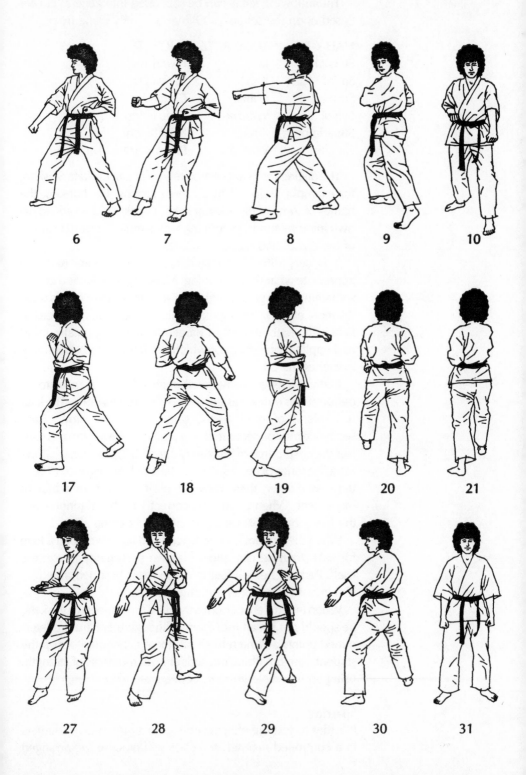

6 7 8 9 10

17 18 19 20 21

27 28 29 30 31

The following katas can be separated into general classes based upon the school of Okinawa-te they came from:–

NAHA-TE	TOMARI-TE	SHURI-TE
Seienchin	Jitte	Bassai Sho
Saifa	Jion	Bassai Dai
Seishan	Rohei	Chinto
Seipai	Wanshu	Goju Shiho
Suparimpei	Jiin	Nai Hanchi
Sanchin	Wankan	Pinan Katas

The distinction is not completely clear and the kata Seishan, for example, is found in all three groups. In changing the names of some of the ancient katas, Funakoshi also added his own interpretations, producing for example, a distinct variant of the Bassai Sho Kata.

It is very difficult for students practising kata really to appreciate what they are doing. Many regard kata as a chore; something to be got through with so as to be able to pass on to the more exciting free fighting. This is a great shame, since the kata is the embodiment of Karate-do, teaching a calm mind and application – both of which are integral to becoming a master of the art.

Many students behave as though a kata is a race; to be performed as quickly as possible. This is quite wrong. The kata is a blend of movements, some fast, some slow. Each sequence may be separated by a pause, as the karateka visualises the next source of imaginary attack. In the stillness following a fast series of moves, the karateka swivels his head to 'see' the new danger, then throws himself forwards in a blur of movement. When performed correctly in this manner, even the lowly basic katas such as the Pinans come alive.

When the student is experienced and has developed a love for kata, then he can allow his own personality to express itself. Perhaps he will feel that a move is best performed by him in a slightly shorter, or longer stance.

When the student performs the hard movements of the kata, he should put his all into them. Although there are predetermined points at which to shout, there is nothing to stop the student from breathing out suddenly, at moments of strength, using an inaudible grunt to concentrate force.

Sparring
In order to test the effectiveness of techniques and counters in a controlled manner, the class will practise pre-arranged

sparring. In its simplest form, this can involve an attacker taking three steps, each accompanied by an attack, with the defender retreating from the first two but countering the third. A much faster variant involves a single pre-arranged attacking step with immediate counter. In modern Karate dojos, this latter form is now often practised in a 'free style format'. This is to say that the attacking technique is put in hard and once delivered, the attacker does not wait around for the defender to work out what to do.

Some schools go on to develop a whole series of free style attacking moves, with a kick for instance, followed by a reverse punch, which, in turn, is followed by a roundhouse kick. The defender's response to each component of the attack will be arranged and demand a high degree of skill. The highest form of pre-arranged sparring is called 'Jiyu Ippon'. This is virtually free fighting except that the attacker and the set attack are known beforehand.

At some stage in the evening's practice, the instructor will call 'Jiyu Kumite!' This is free fighting, where the basic and combination techniques so diligently practised are put into a muted kind of action. In some clubs, students are not allowed to fight until they have mastered the basic techniques. This is a logical and sensible way to proceed. There is no point in getting a student to kick, for instance, if he has not mastered the art of pulling the toes back.

It is a fact that many injuries in Karate occur during free fighting and especially when a higher grade is fighting a lower grade. Because of the wide intake into Karate, there are quite a few instructors and higher grades who do not have the correct mental approach. When fighting with the lower grades, they do not encourage the spirit of the lower grade by providing openings, or using slow techniques. They try, instead, to knock the lower grades about, as though to reinforce their weak egos. Such clubs and higher grades should be avoided.

During free fighting, some clubs allow the use of fist and shin/instep protectors. These are thin layers of pliable foam which fold over the bones, so as to minimise the effect of impact. Too much padding, though, is definitely a bad thing and encourages the fighter to attack hard when there is no target.

Head injury is not peculiar to Karate, it occurs in all martial arts. In the striking arts, it occurs when a blow knocks the head back, even slightly. In such cases, the brain bangs against the front of the skull and may become bruised. One or two even lightish impacts can result in brain damage and this may well show up in the form of headaches, or inability to concentrate.

If ever a student receives a bang in the head whilst training, he should stop immediately and ask for permission to quit the class. Provided there are no serious symptoms, such as double vision, or passing out, he will probably be alright as long as he does not engage in further sparring, or activity likely to cause another bang in the head for a period of not less than six weeks.

Karate competition

With the coming of the Meiji period, the old caste distinctions became blurred and the exclusive right of the Samurai to bear arms was overturned in favour of conscript armies consisting of people who ordinarily would never have been trained in a martial art. Into this period came Karate, a martial art devised by the peasants of Okinawa. The Japanese government became aware of the use to which such arts could be put, even in modern warfare and so large numbers of conscripts were trained in their use.

Outside Japan, one of the main factors leading to Karate's rapid uptake was the possibility of fighting and competition. The Japan Karate Association developed the first accepted form of free fighting in the nineteen-thirties, though others had tried various methods even before then. Fights with boxing gloves and Kendo armour presented one alternative but it was the 'semi contact' of the JKA that became the widely accepted norm and the base from which developed true competition in the 1950s.

Before the advent of systematised free fighting, there had been numerous clandestine duels between different schools and these were often bloody affairs. The imposition of a widely accepted set of rules meant that people fought on the same terms and started from a position of equal advantage. In all free fighting, the object is to test the student against an opponent. In the process of doing so, he is not expected to kill or maim the other person. Therefore certain types of technique have to be ruled out because of the danger their usage poses. As an example, from the earliest times, spear hand attacks to the eyes were ruled out.

Not only Karate, but other arts have felt that once an acceptable form of fighting with rules is imposed, the art itself suffers. This has certainly been the case with Karate and modern karateka often regard their ability as being measured by success in the competition arena. On the other hand, all those arts which have embraced fighting or competition, can report continuing expansion in their membership, thus indicating more interest in competition than art.

Be that as it may, since early days Karate competition has been highly regarded by the majority of karateka practising throughout the world. The initial form of competition was called the 'Shobuippon', or 'single point' type of match. In this system, the fighters warily circled each other until an opening was created or seen, whereupon a single attack was made. If that single attack was regarded as effective, then the attacker was awarded the 'Ippon', or 'definitive point'.

The theory behind this was that in a real fight, there was only the possibility of one effective attack, after which the opponent would be killed, or mortally wounded. The attacking technique had to be carefully controlled, so that it did not actually cause injury and one of the sad paradoxes of Karate competition was to see the winner being wheeled away on a stretcher – as a result of a foul blow landing hard!

From the spectator's point of view, the Shobuippon form of competition was dull, with little action and no spectacular technique. Even the incorporation of the Waza-ari, or 'scoring technique' (awarded half a point despite being required to have the technical content amounting to ninety per cent of an ippon) afforded little visual improvement.

In an effort to encourage more difficult techniques and to have a more open competition format, the World Union Of Karate Organisations introduced Sanbon Shobu, or 'three ippon competition'. This system allowed more opportunity for the fighters to display their skill. No longer did a single error mean loss of the bout. The waza-ari was dropped and there was a clamp down on contact – especially to the head and face. The latter move proved to be unwise.

An unwelcome outcome of the 'no contact' rule was a totally unmartial art-like, but thoroughly sensible mis-use of the rules called 'tactical diving'. This disgraceful phenomenon involves the faking of injury caused by the opponent's technique, so that the latter gets penalised, or is even disqualified from the bout!

Quite recently, the rules have changed again and whilst the Sanbon Kumite system has been kept, waza-aris have been reintroduced, allowing a possible score of up to six good techniques in any bout. This is a tacit acknowledgment that sport karate has finally arrived. The reintroduction of a certain degree of face contact and the penalisation of tactical diving may well lead to an improvement. One cannot, however, visualise a Karate match after Funakoshi, i.e. stepping inside someone's attack and seizing his testicles. Though beautifully effective, it is not sport!

Oyama of the Kyokushinkai has derided the WUKO style competition, describing it as a 'dance'. His Knockdown Competition is an attempt to return to a martial art image but it suffers from its own rules just as badly as the WUKO's. The constant hacking away at legs means that very often, Kyokushinkai Competitions are won by those who are not necessarily better but are merely more able to absorb punishment. The fact that the bout is not stopped unless there actually is a knockdown means that the spectacular high kicks, beloved of spectators, are dangerous to use because, if ineffective, they leave the kicker open to counter-attack. The prohibition on face punching leads to fighting from an unrealistic distance, whilst making no attempt to guard the

Karate competition area

1. White (Shiro) contestant's standing line (1 m)
2. Judge's standing line (½ m)
3. Red (Aka) contestant's standing line
4. Referee's standing line
5. 6 metre inner square
6. 8 metre outer square
7. Safety area
8. Arbitrator's chair
9. Area control table
10. Scorekeeper
11. Timekeeper

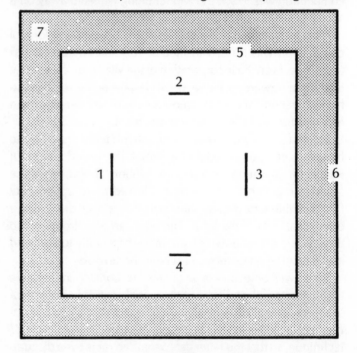

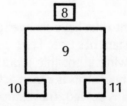

face which is, of course, a prime target in any real fight.

Now that it has become more widely accepted, even by the Japanese themselves, that sport karate is a distinct activity within the overall framework, the stage has been set for new and exciting future developments in this area. It is possible that the present form of team competition will be replaced by one in which the individual fighters are matched by weight. The individual bouts of Karate matches already use weight divisions and the common ones now in use are:–

WOMEN: Minimum weight 43 kilos (95 lbs.)

–53 Kilos (116 lbs.)	–60 Kilos (132 lbs.)	Over 60 Kilos
(Lightweight)	(Middleweight)	(Heavyweight)

MEN: Under 18 years (Junior)

–60 Kilos (132 lbs.)	–65 Kilos (143 lbs.)	–70 Kilos (154 lbs.)
(Super-Lightweight)	(Lightweight)	(Middleweight)
–75 Kilos (165 lbs.)	Over 75 Kilos	
(Light-Heavyweight)	(Heavyweight)	

Over 18 years (Seniors)

–60 Kilos (132 lbs.)	–65 Kilos (143 lbs.)	–70 Kilos (154 lbs.)
(Super-Lightweight)	(Lightweight)	(Light-Middleweight)
–75 Kilos (165 lbs.)	–80 Kilos (176 lbs.)	Over 80 Kilos
(Middleweight)	(Light-Heavyweight)	(Heavyweight)
	Open Weight (Any weight)	

There is a possibility that future Karate competition will continue the trend of contact and though never amounting to Full Contact a greater allowance will be permitted. Already there is a trend towards quite substantial body contact and this is sure to produce a more athletic, conditioned body than is currently required. There may well be a development of the present system of stratified scoring – where a scheduled and skillful technique tends to receive a higher score than a more simple, or easily executed one. At present, the system has two tiers – a fighter can score either a full point, or a half point. Later systems may move to a three tier arrangement, with top marks awarded for a very technically difficult technique, such as a throw and follow-through.

One of the latest ideas is that of using a microchip to compare the inputs fed to it by a panel of judges, doing in a microsecond what it currently takes a panel of judges considerably longer to do. By these means, sport Karate will move further and further away from the martial art roots, becoming ever more a combat sport.

5. KEMPO

Shorinji Kempo

The art of Shorinji Kempo is rather curious, claiming as it does to have descended from the Chinese martial art of the Shaolin Temple. The name itself is a Japanese reading of Shaolinsu-Chuanfa, the latter term simply meaning 'boxing'. The founder of the system was known as Doshin So, the first name being a Chinese reading of his personal name.

Doshin So was born Michiomi Nakano, the son of a member of Japan's nationalistic Black Dragon Society. Nakano's father died when he was young and so he was sent to Manchuria, to live with his grandfather. On the subsequent death of the grandfather, Nakano returned to Japan where he himself joined the Black Dragon Society. He returned to Manchuria in 1928, in order to spy for the Japanese Government. Whilst there, he began to study Chinese martial art under a Chinese priest.

During his spying operations, he travelled extensively through China and eventually came to Peking, where he met Wen Lou-Shi, a grand master of one of the Northern Shaolin styles of Chinese martial art known as I-He Chuan. Wen is believed to have studied at the Sungshan Shaolin monastery. Nakano trained under the master and was shown a wall scroll when he visited the Shaolin Temple. The scroll was an inspiration and helped him formulate the basis for Shorinji Kempo and Kongo-Zen.

His martial art training in China was interrupted when the Russians overran Manchuria and he was obliged to flee the country, returning to Japan. He studied Daito Ryu Aiki Jiu Jitsu and became proficient in the art before leaving to devise his own system, which he called Nippon Densei To Shorinji Kempo, so as to distinguish it from the other, pre-existing schools of Kempo. Kempo is a fairly common expression in Japanese and means any form of striking system which has a connection with China.

At the heart of Shorinji Kempo is the Kongo-Zen philosophy. Kongo-Zen means 'having a mind like a diamond'. Using this philosophy, followers concentrate on the concept of self-help, avoiding a reliance upon others, or the intervention of a Godhead. The top instructors of Shorinji Kempo are monks who wear a dark robe over their white training tunics. This robe is tied by means of a thick, round belt. During each lesson, there is a period of quiet, seated meditation, where the class all sit cross legged in regular lines. One student moves amongst those seated, using a staff which is placed against their backs. The seated student will then straighten and adjust his posture until it is upright. At the conclusion of meditation, the pole is rapped smartly against the floor, producing a sudden sharp noise in the otherwise still training hall.

Techniques

The seated meditation takes place at a mid point in the training session. First is exercise, then the practice of basic technique which, as in Karate, are called 'Kihon'. The punches are all quickly withdrawn after the blow and whilst there is a certain degree of hiptwist, the fist does not rotate on impact. The punches and kicks are taught together with avoidance techniques. These involve head movements and evasions. Blocks are taught together with counters, so as not to isolate the one from the other.

The kicks, like the punches, are performed with a snap action, thus giving extra impact. All the normal complement are used, including front kicks, roundhouse kicks and sidekick. In all cases, these are delivered only to weak points of the opponent's anatomy. There are also simple exchanges of basic techniques between practising pairs and this is referred to as 'Pair-Form Kihon'. Combination techniques increase fluidity and Aikido-like roll outs complete this part of the syllabus.

The second part of the syllabus involves what are called 'Juho', or compliant techniques (the first part dealt with the 'Goho' or hard techniques). In this section are some three hundred locks and throws, many of which are identical to the techniques of Jiu Jitsu and Aikido. There are evasions, wrist-locks and armlocks and all usually prefaced with a strike to the opponent's weak points. The higher teaching grades are taught the use of 'Atemi-Waza' (special techniques which can cause unconsciousness, paralysis, or death) but this teaching is verbal only and there are no readily available written manuals. By a light blow to the right spot, the expert in atemi-waza can paralyse or even knock out the strongest assailant.

The basic techniques of juho and goho are taught by senior grades who train with the lower grades. This is a good method of teaching for both, since the junior student receives one-to-one attention and the senior student gains a new insight into the technique by teaching it to another and correcting his mistakes. As a result of this intensive partner training, the

The 'Gassho' is the method of salutation used in Shorinji Kempo

This illustration shows how Shorinji Kempo incorporates both joint locking holds and strikes

Shorinji Kempo student develops an early awareness of the value of his partner.

This respect is very much in evidence in the performance of what are called 'Embus'. These are lifelike sequences of sparring, lasting for two minutes and consisting of four or five sequences. The embus involve a balance of goho and juho techniques and each one is rehearsed so that both partners know exactly what is happening. The idea of the pre-arranged embu is to demonstrate perfect form in a fast moving situation. Whilst embus are required for grading examinations, more advanced students are encouraged to make up their own. In the embu, each partner takes it in turn to go through the sequence as attacker and defender.

A similar concept underlies the practising of kata, though the pace is not so furious. Each kata may be performed singly, or with a partner. There are eight katas for the kyu grades and they are performed to a count. Each kata contains around ten moves, with the first five constituting a series of attacks and the latter five, a series of defence moves.

During the course of the training, there will also be a discussion on some technical or philosophical point. Aspects of Kongo-Zen are taught to lower grades by simple rote learning and it is only when one reaches higher grades, that an individual understanding is sought. On the technical side, any topic of Shorinji Kempo technique may come in for analysis. A popular subject is the theory of attack. The Shorinji Kempo student is advised to select a specific target, rather than just flail away. In order for an attack to be successful, correct distancing is essential, so body positioning becomes a major factor. The angle of attack is also important, since the direction of movement of one student relative to another may well mask the selected target. Use is often made of this concept during evasion and counter-attacking.

Speed of attack is another vital component and strategy suggests that it be used when the opponent is least expecting it. Skilled students listen to their opponents breathing and when the breath is sucked in, then they will attack. Randori is practised between the more senior grades and it permits little contact, with none at all to the head or groin areas. When randori occurs, it involves either juho, or goho techniques but never both. There have been a small number of competitions but these are purely for interest's sake. There are no prizes and no awarding of places since this is contrary to the spirit of Shorinji Kempo.

Skilled exponents of the art often use knowledge of vital points in a beneficial way. A controlled pressure on these can have a healing effect. This healing massage is known as 'Seiho' and it is by no means peculiar to Shorinji Kempo. Practised under different names, it is also found in some schools of Karate and Jiu Jitsu. It is also, of course, a major part of the advanced syllabus for many Chinese martial art systems. There is one substantiated case on record where a student of another discipline collapsed during training and an instructor of Shorinji Kempo was near at hand. Invited to look at the stricken student, he quickly recognised the symptoms of heart block and with a blow of his hand to the back, restarted the heart beating!

There are five kyu grades in Shorinji Kempo, starting with the white belt, then going to yellow, green, blue and finally brown. There is an interval of six months between gradings and between brown belt and black belt, a minimum period of a year must be spent revising techniques. During this time, the student will be required to take three oaths, the first being 'Seiku' ('Pledge'), the second 'Seigan' ('Holy Maxim') and the third, 'Shinjo' ('Creed'). When the student finally becomes a black belt, he will be entitled to wear the dark, over-tunic and tubular belt.

Analysing Shorinji Kempo from the outside, it is very difficult to see the Chinese influence. The practice is very much Japanese in nature, with the characteristic snap kicks using the ball of the foot being much in evidence. The juho techniques are astonishingly similar to those used in Aiki Jiu Jitsu and the overall discipline and etiquette are typical of the dojos of other Japanese martial art ways. Even the greeting, or 'Gassho' is quite distinctly Japanese, the hands being held high in front of the face, rather than lower down at chest level. More curious for a supposed Shaolin based system is the absence of Chinese weapons from the training routine.

From this, the onlooker is bound to form the opinion that this system is very far from being a Chinese martial art. This view has been apparently shared by other parties, who won a

Shorinji Kempo uses fast strikes to vulnerable targets

court action resulting in So amending the name of his system to 'Nippon Shorinji Kempo', or 'Japanese Shaolin Boxing'. The founder has since died and the head of Shorinji Kempo is Doshin So's daughter. She is assisted by the senior instructors of the main training establishment at Chikoku, an island just off the coast of Japan.

It is claimed that a Shorinji Kempo branch operates in Peking and if so, then it is the only foreign martial art so allowed. It has been suggested that such a link could serve as an informal channel of communications between Peking and Tokyo.

Nippon Kempo

Nippon Kempo differs from many of the other arts in that it does not have a long lineage going back to Okinawa, or China. It is a uniquely Japanese activity, created by Muneumi Sawayama in 1932. Sawayama was a student of Judo and joined the Karatedo class of Kansai University as a student. One of his major interests was in developing a form of safe combat sport and with this in mind, he devised the system of Nippon Kempo, or 'Japanese Fistway'.

In devising the system, he took techniques from the various schools of Karate, Judo and Aikido. The wearing of armour is an integral part of competitive sparring. This armour is similar to that used in Kendo in that there is a head protector with a steel face grill, a breast-plate and gloves.

The head protector or men resembles a catcher's mask more than the Kendo men. Because there is no narrow shinai to poke through into the face, the grillwork is much wider. The throat flap is also reduced in size, since it does not have to deflect a thrust to the throat. Beneath the head protector, not one but three separate head bands are used to cushion the head against impact. One winds around the forehead, the other around the temples and the third, around the jaw. This substantial padding is certain to remove virtually all possibility of laceration to the protected area but there remains the danger of brain injury caused by thumps to the head. Even when cushioned, the acceleration of the head by a blow can cause the brain to impact against the skull.

The chest protector is known as the Do, just as in Kendo. It is made of polished fibreglass, curved to fit around the sides. To protect the body from severe impact, a padded jacket is worn under the gi jacket. This waistcoat is known as the Dobuton.

Nippon Kempo fighters compete in full armour

The groin protector, or kin is worn over the gi pants and boxing gloves are worn on the hands. Sawayama was not the only one investigating ways of sparring in armour. The notable Okinawan Karate master Shinken Taira also used boxing gloves during the nineteen-thirties but in full contact Karate competition. Old photographs show him wearing shoulder and arm pads, plus a padded jacket and padded overtrousers.

The Nippon Kempo gi itself is usually the same as a karate-gi and the different standards of students are identified by a system of coloured belts. Each belt refers to a specific Kyu, or grade of achievement. Grading examinations are held in principle every three months though this time may be varied to accommodate different levels of aptitude. The belt colours are as follows:–

White   Beginner
Yellow   8th Kyu
Orange   7th Kyu
Green   6th & 5th Kyu
Blue   4th & 3rd Kyu
Brown   2nd & 1st Kyu
Black   1st–10th Dan

A very strict hierarchy is observed during training. The class senior is known as the Sempai and the instructor is Sensei. The junior grade is referred to as 'Kohai'. To the 8th kyu, the 7th kyu is Sempai and so on, up the scale. The idea of this system is to instil respect for fellow students. Reinforcing this is an exclamation which is made during practice. The exclamation is Osu, generally pronounced 'Uhs'.

The meaning of this word is vague but it signifies respect. Thus, when entering a training hall, or 'Dojo', the student will look towards the instructor, or in his absence the sempai and salute them with the osu. Before sparring, or when practising with a partner, osu is voiced, indicating a desire to practise with respect and in the hope of learning. Good manners dictate the use of osu when seeking to leave the training hall, when arriving late for training and seeking admission to the class. It is also used if the student has to stop training for any reason.

This insistence on politeness and the cultivation of respect indicates that Nippon Kempo is not merely a sport but a character building exercise, in the tradition of the 'Do', or 'way'. There appears to be a great deal of dispute over the nature of the do and whether it can be incorporated into a system with sporting links. The martial art way of Aikido will say that it cannot, whilst some of its own schools disagree. Kendo is the oldest of the Japanese martial art ways and yet it too contains a sporting principle.

Nippon Kempo advises the student to practise outside the dojo, improving his techniques so they may be corrected during formal lessons. There are two types of techniques, the striking and the grappling. Grappling techniques are taught to 4th Kyu and above. They consist of armlocks (eleven varieties) and throws (thirteen). Grappling is practised as a part of Hogeki Kata, where two partners will take it in turns alternately to attack and then allow attack. 'Ukemi' or break-falls are taught as part of the syllabus.

The striking techniques are based upon very fast movements which utilise a snapping action in their delivery. There is emphasis on focus, with the muscles tightening spasmodically on impact. Since Nippon Kempo is not a full contact sport, the blows do not have to land heavily and so insistence is laid upon perfect form during delivery. The striking techniques do not merely involve the direct strikes, familiar to the student of Karate, they also involve swinging and hooking punches. As with Shorinji Kempo, the blows are taught and practised in conjunction with evasion and counters. There are six separate evasion techniques, involving the simple duck and side to side movements of the head and body. Foot movement is taught as a separate syllabus item, with close attention paid to the rapid changing of stance.

The syllabus reflects the nature of Nippon Kempo. There is no heavy, rooted to the ground approach that one finds in the sanchin stance of Okinawan Karate schools. Nippon Kempo teaches the light, weaving movements which look very much like a systematised analysis of western boxing. Indeed, one of the practice methods recommended by the school is to 'shadow box'. This has been used in some of the competition oriented styles of Karate and found to be very beneficial. A mirror is a very useful thing to use since it shows weaknesses and openings in the guard. Shadow boxing, or 'Soran' as it is called, greatly improves fluidity and allows basic techniques to be strung together into a natural sequence.

'Kuran' is a fast form of no-contact sparring used by Nippon Kempo students to gain knowledge of distance and strategy. No matter how much shadow boxing is done, it cannot teach how to deal with an opponent with tactics and ideas of his own. Kuran allows this concept to be felt out, yet without injury to either partner. During kuran, the student learns to put evasion, blocks and counters into action. After a while, practice leads onto sparring in armour, or 'Bogu Renshu'. In this form, blows of strictly limited force may be landed and during close work, throws and locks are employed. If one of the students is thrown, the fight may continue in a form of groundwork which is brought to a stop when an effective technique is scored.

During competition, knee, elbow, shin and instep padding may be worn. The latter is no doubt useful in reducing injury caused by the instep connecting the faceguard. Only full points, or 'Ippon' are awarded and each bout continues for two minutes. There are no weight classes in use because impact of a heavy nature is frowned upon. The best fighters are those who have learned techniques and tactics so well that they no longer have to concentrate on them. Their minds are clear and able to react without conscious effort or thought. In Nippon Kempo, this state of mind is known as 'Mushin'.

In 1977, Sawayama died at the age of seventy-two. He is replaced by his lifelong friend and student, Fumio Yano 10th dan. Nippon Kempo is currently practised in Great Britain, the USA, Japan, Korea and Zambia. All the satellite groups have close connections with the Japanese Honbu ('Main Dojo'), sending there their senior grades for advanced training.

CHINA

KUNG FU

History

The word 'Kung Fu,' or 'Gung Fu' merely means 'good effort', or 'well done!' It does not translate as Chinese martial art, though common usage has led it to mean just that. Even Chinese themselves now use the name 'Kung Fu'. Purists would probably call the Chinese martial arts 'Wu Shu', with the unarmed varieties (sometimes called Chinese Boxing) being referred to as 'Chuanfa' (Fist Way), 'Tang Shou ('Hand of Tang'), or 'Chuan Shu'.

Owing to the low degree of literacy of the Chinese peasant and the effect that long periods of time and violent upheavals have had on such records as may have existed, it will come as no surprise to learn that the origins of Chinese martial art are obscure. One school of thought says that the Shaolin Temple was responsible and another considers that the art was already present by the time the Temple was set up.

China has had a very long history of civilisation with much conflict and war. It seems rather silly therefore, to imagine that no techniques, or schools of martial art predate the Shaolin Temple. There is little doubt, however, that the Temple did have a major effect upon the martial arts.

The existence of the Temple is in no doubt because it can still be found in the Hunan Province of China. It suffered damage in 1674, when it was put to the torch by a cautious emperor who didn't much like the idea of a group of expert warriors operating outside his control. In 1928 it was burnt down again, this time by the marauding forces of a local warlord. Despite these two calamities, the wall paintings have survived, though all of the written material has been destroyed.

Some Chinese scholars believe that there may have been more than one Shaolin Temple, with another site possibly in Fukien. Although no evidence can be found to support this belief, in a land as large as China, it seems strange that there should have been only one Buddhist temple.

The Temple at Hunan was built for an Indian monk; one of

several who made the perilous journey from Northern India to bring the teachings of the Buddha. The existing Chinese religion was based upon the teachings of Confucius and Lao Tzu and many Chinese understandably opposed the introduction of a foreign religion. Nevertheless, Buddhism did manage to gain an entry and was accepted even to the point of monarchs allocating land and materials to construct a temple.

One of the most famed of the Indian monks to visit China was Bhodidharma. It seems very likely that he gained admission to the Hunan Temple in the early part of the sixth century. Bhodidharma ('Ta Mo', in Chinese and 'Daruma' in Japanese) introduced a new concept of Buddhism to China, which involved very long periods of static meditation. This form of Buddhism was known as 'Chan' ('Zen' in Japanese). It encouraged the disciple to seek enlightenment from within, rather than looking outwards towards idols. Bhodidharma taught that God is to be found within.

The idea of Zen spread throughout the Far East, carried by Buddhist monks who journeyed into Korea and Japan in early times. In those countries, 'hard' martial arts developed; 'hard' meaning that a great deal of force was used in their techniques. It is interesting to note that in Japan, the underlying theme of Zen was associated with extremely rigorous and forceful martial arts which were 'softened' when the Tokugawa Shoguns introduced the study of Taoism. From this time on, 'soft' techniques began to appear in greater numbers involving 'compliant', or 'yielding' techniques.

Bhodidharma found the monks of the Shaolin Temple unable to adopt the rigorous meditation required by Zen and so he suggested two sets of exercises to help them. One was called 'The Exchange of Ligament' and the other, 'Washing the Marrow'. It has been suggested that he also taught a pattern ('Kata' in Japanese) called the 'Eighteen Lohan'. Early records seem to show the existence of a pattern at this time but it used only hand techniques, with no kicks. It seems likely that some of the monks may have already had some knowledge of Chinese martial art and its fusion with Zen may have led to sudden development.

With the establishment of training at the Shaolin Temple, came such things as practice schedules. Contemporary texts describe a two hour early morning training session, an early afternoon and an evening session. Senior students were also given a midnight session. The juniors were taught in groups, using a courtyard. Depressions worn into the stone from the

Bhodidharma (Ta No in Chinese) is widely regarded as the originator of Shaolin Kung Fu

feet of countless students seem to confirm this use. Senior students received personal tuition and had to undergo an initiation ceremony before they could leave the Temple as an expert. This ceremony does not appear to be the same as that shown on the television – lifting a red hot urn with the forearms – though that might perhaps have been the requirement in other temples. In Hunan, the seniors were required to fight their way through five separate gates, each one defended by a master.

By the seventh century AD the Temple housed over one thousand monks, a large proportion of which were actively training in martial art. A civil disturbance led the emperor of that time to call upon the monks for aid. They supplied a small force of fighting men and helped him to put down the disturbance, returning afterwards to the Temple to continue with their devotions. In return for their aid, the emperor granted the Temple the right to train a force of warrior monks.

The warrior monks have been prevalent also in Japan, where they sometimes served as bodyguards and tutors. In Korea also, warrior monks were implicated in the introduction of new techniques to the existing martial art forms. It could well be that they had a similar role in Okinawa, giving rise eventually to Karate. Current thinking suggests that at least one of the inputs to Karate did come from one of the various hard styles practised in the Shaolin Temple.

The Chinese warrior monks of the Tang dynasty might well have led to use of the term 'Tang Shou', or 'Hand of Tang'. This title is significant in that it appears in Korea under the title 'Tang Soo Do', or 'Way of the Tang Hand' and of course in the original writing of Karate, which meant 'China (Tang) Hand'.

The growing expertise and reputation of the warrior monks no doubt led to their downfall. In a subsequent conflict, the monks were asked for aid and gave it. This time, the Emperor Kang Hsi saw with his own eyes the tremendous fighting power of the monks and decided to eliminate them. In the ensuing fight, all but five warrior monks were slain, these

Practice with the spear occurs in several schools of Kung Fu. It is a relic of battlefield practice

latter being referred to now as 'The Five Ancestors'. They gave rise to the five major classic Shaolin styles found today which are Lau, Hung Gar, Choy, Lai and Mok. Many subsequent schools of Shaolin art have arisen from a combination, or fusion of these ancestral types, so that it is impossible to say now just how many schools of Chinese Shaolin martial art there are.

The five monks split up and went their separate ways. Some may have gone to other temples, whilst the others remained with the ruins of the Hunan Temple. The Temple was rebuilt, following the reign of Kang Hsi and efforts were made to recreate the wall murals which showed Indian and Chinese monks practising together. In 1928, the Temple fell into disuse, its monks scattered by the internecine warring. With the coming of the communists, many fled the mainland, taking refuge in Taiwan and Hong Kong. Some remained and were allowed to return to the Temple. No new monks have been allowed to join and the Temple has been restored as a curio.

The scattering of the monks may have been significant to the spread of systematised Shaolin martial art. If there were no other Shaolin temples teaching warrior monks, then the split up would have been very important; whereas if there were many such temples, then the effect would have been minimal. During their wanderings, it is said that the monks studied animal movement and extracted its essence to add to their existing knowledge. They had studied under several masters whilst in the Temple and the distinctions between the various styles may have already begun to blur at this point.

There are several legends concerned with the development of a new system based on the movement of animals. The crane, or stork would appear to have been a most quarrelsome creature if every such story is to be believed. Some saw it fighting snakes, as in the case of the nun Ng Mui, the founder of Wing Chun. Others saw it fighting with an ape, or a bear and devised Peh Hoke from that. By way of a change, the founder of Monkey Style was imprisoned in a jail guarded by fierce monkeys. He managed to escape by mimicking their movements so skilfully that they mistook him for one of them! This sort of story abounds in Chinese martial art folklore. There are also instances where whole systems were literally 'dreamed up' by the odd sleeping monk.

A favourite story concerns a group of monks who got tipsy through eating over-ripe fruit (sic) and then found themselves having to defend their lives in a fierce skirmish with would-be

The fighter on the right attacks with a straight punch. The opponent blocks with the edge of his wrist

robbers. Trained to perfection, their bodies knew exactly how to act, even without their brains directing them. Unfortunately, alcohol has a disturbing effect upon coordination and the monks were staggering and falling all over the place! Apparently, these random movements threw the attackers off completely and the monks were able to subdue them before laying down to sleep it off. From this amusing little story comes the alleged background to the so called 'Drunken Form' that is found in several Shaolin styles.

The monks did teach lay people their art. As an example of this, the Nun Ng Mui taught a Shaolin system to a beautiful young maiden who was to be married off in order to relieve a family debt. The maiden's name was 'Wing Chun', which means 'Beautiful Springtime'. One can only wonder how long the training took and for how long she was able to put off the despised marriage! Another style taught to the public was named after its founder's nickname. The monk 'Pak Mei' (White Eyebrows) was famous for the size and bushiness of his eyebrows, as well as for his great skill in Shaolin.

When the Shaolin arts became well known, individual villages sought to retain the services of a trained martial artist. This person not only functioned as a local sheriff, he also doubled as the village bonesetter. Properly trained Shaolin martial artists were not only skilled in damaging people, they were equally skilled in mending them again afterwards using

The opponent then looses a front kick which is parried. Note the defender's face guard

The defender simultaneously blocks a strike delivered upon landing and counters to the eyes

herbs, poultices and natural medicines. If the martial artist had been trained under a non-Shaolin tradition the healing treatment would have involved using the meridians, or channels along which that person's 'Chi' ('Ki' in Japanese) or life force, flowed.

The local teachers taught the village families and the families in turn passed on knowledge to their sons and daughters. In this way, still further variation was introduced. Secret techniques were evolved and jealously guarded by the particular family that devised them. There are very many such family styles, the majority of which are just not known.

Another factor to consider in the development of Chinese martial art is the immense size of the country. It is a well known biological fact that variations in physical characteristics occur with the passage of time. When the country is small and the population compact, these variations soon spread throughout the whole and everyone experiences the change together. In a widely spread population, however, any variation occurring in a region may not be passed throughout the whole but remain localised. As time passes, the variation may follow a trend, becoming more and more pronounced. This very thing may have happened with some of the schools of Chinese martial art.

Supposing a single style is introduced to a spread out area, with little knots of population here and there. In one area, the peasants work the land, tilling the ground and carrying bales of cereal produce. Because of their strong arm and back muscles, they may prefer the hand techniques of that style and spend more time working at these than practising with kicks. In another part of the country, the people live in a very mountainous area and work at tending sheep. Because of the hilly pastures and the distance to be covered each day, their legs are very strong and supple and so they concentrate on the kicking parts of the same martial art system.

After a period of time, in which competitions are held and development pursued, the two areas will have changed the system so far from what they were both taught that it looks almost as if they are practising two different styles entirely. Such a theory as this is commonly advanced to explain the existence of two categories of Shaolin martial art. There are the Northern styles, which involve much leg work and are noted for their open stances and rapid movements and there are the Southern styles which in contrast are typically 'closed', relying mainly upon the arms and strong stances. These latter styles are thought to have contributed to the development of Okinawan Karate.

Of course, there will be exceptions to every rule and the individual master of a Southern style may have good legs and emphasize this in his teaching. There may also be a master of

The Wing Chun Punch is a short, jolting move which travels only a few inches

the Northern style who is of heavy build and therefore not suited to light, airy movements. The common factor though with all Shaolin systems, is a preponderance of hard technique. This has been discussed generally before but will now be examined in greater detail.

The Hard Systems of Kung Fu

It is possible to meet force with force. When that happens the greater of the two forces will normally win. By introducing blocks and counters, the lesser force can prevail as long as the user is adequately skilled. In Shaolin techniques, the strikes are made with great power. Sometimes this power is generated, as in Karate, by the withdrawal of the non striking limb and attendant hiptwist. Other times, the hip is not used and the attacker moves in behind a very short range punch with the arm held rigid like a billiard cue. In both cases there are strong muscle movements, especially of the upper body.

One way of developing this power is to stand relaxed and then suddenly imagine that you have been tickled. The all-over spasm of the muscles which it produces is exactly that used in the short range punches which make some styles of Chinese martial art so effective. The fist is often used with the thumb upwards – as is the case in some Okinawan schools. In other styles, the fist rocks on impact, with the index knuckle impacting first, followed in turn by all the lower knuckles.

One particular style happened to use a special 'vibrating' fist which was supposed to be highly effective. When an unbeliever asked for a demonstration, the punch was shown, gingerly at first, on his stomach. When no effect was seen, a harder blow was used and when this too produced no response, the class senior was ordered over to sort things out. With an almighty punch, which was presumably vibrating, the blow deflected off the unbeliever's belly and the class senior ended up in the rose bed! This little anecdote serves to illustrate the fact that students, when taking up a Chinese martial art, have no real way of knowing if the art they are studying is genuine. With the craze for Kung Fu, people saw a chance to make money and so, overnight, became masters of little known Kung Fu styles of which no-one had ever previously heard.

The great secrecy that surrounds the teaching of authentic Chinese martial art ensures that only the tip of the iceberg is seen. Many of the real masters will not teach outsiders even today. It is true that there are some who will but even these will only teach a diluted form. Usually, a master will only teach one or two pupils the true essence of that school.

Limb conditioning is well known in the Shaolin styles and there are tales of schools hardening their hands to an incredible degree. In most cases, a simple wooden dummy is made. This is roughly man height and is composed of a semi smoothed tree trunk from which projects spars at various heights representing limbs. More modern Shaolin schools use stainless steel and plastic dummies, for such is progress! The trunk and the spars are struck in a sequence of moves which calls into action the knuckles, elbows, finger tips, forearms and soles of feet. To ease the bruising that takes place during such training, various medicines are rubbed in. Eventually, the sensation in these parts becomes dulled and it is then possible to smash the dummy with great force.

Styles that favour open hand techniques spend vast amounts of training time, thrusting the hand into sand, or pebbles. There are records of some schools who repeatedly plunge their hands into bowls of red hot iron balls! If this is supplemented by applying astringents and lotions, the whole hand can become like a horny claw. To coincide with this hand conditioning, the student can also wield a very heavy staff and by swishing it through the air and abruptly stopping it, the arms and chest muscles can be strengthened to a

The Wing Chun Kick uses the heel of the foot to attack low targets

remarkable degree. Yet another exercise is throwing a large and irregular heavy stone into the air and catching it with a snatching motion. The result of years of this kind of training is to make the arms strong enough literally to tear the flesh from a person's bones! Outstretched fingers can quite easily spear through clothes and inflict the most frightful damage.

In less extreme schools, such as those of the Praying Mantis, steel bars are rolled along the forearm to the wrists and then flung up high in the air, to be caught on the forearms and rolled back to the wrists again. In this particular style, the forearms are the focus of conditioning since they move like the capturing and crushing arms of the praying mantis. An incoming punch is allowed past the front arm, whereupon the rear forearm moves across and traps the fist. The use of force in the following rear arm block makes it capable of breaking the forearm bones of the puncher!

In the Southern styles, the kicks are invariably kept low and use the heel to deliver the impact. Front and sidekicks are normally directed to the kneecap. In the Northern styles, the kicks are often aimed at the head but when done so, a hand always covers the groin area. Some of the Northern styles jump extremely high and perform flying kicks capable of dislodging a mounted warrior.

To see leaps and bounds in abundance, one has only to see the Chinese Wu Shu Theatre. This twentieth century phenomenon relegates the ancient Chinese martial arts to a gymnastic routine, with pseudo kicks and punches replacing cartwheels and somersaults. The splendid uniforms and clever choreography do not make up for the sad fact that this is what the Chinese mainland feels Wu Shu is all about. Information coming from China seems to indicate that Wu Shu tournaments are now being held containing various 'Style' events. Instead of a true Chinese master, coaches drill their students in the mechanics of the game.

A certain amount of public display has been common to some Kung Fu schools which every year give demonstrations of the Lion Dance. The lion's head is an amazing fabrication of colours and shapes and has a mouth that can be opened and shut by the lead dancer. All lion dancers come from Kung Fu schools and the movements of the beast are highly symbolic. Regrettably, most of the symbolism is lost upon Westerners, though the dance is enjoyed just the same.

The Soft Systems of Kung Fu

The 'soft', or 'internal' Chinese martial arts are held by some to have developed later than the Shaolin, or 'hard' forms. Other scholars point to their use of principles taken from the study of the Tao, which predates Zen Buddhism, suggesting that they appeared earlier than the hard forms. A third opinion suggests that the Shaolin monks originally studied for longer periods and arrived at the soft forms as the ultimate development of the art. When they began to be called upon to produce warriors, the training schedule was shortened and warrior monks who qualified knew only the hard forms.

The latter view is interesting but it does not explain how monks studying Zen Buddhism came to devise an art based upon the principles of Taoist teachings. The two concepts were not regarded as being complementary and there was more than one scuffle between the two religious factions!

The idea of the Tao concerns the driving force of life and the universe. Attempts to describe the concept are thwarted from the outset by such sayings as 'If you are able to describe it, then it is not the Tao!' Regardless of that, the Tao is said to ebb and flow; to circulate in the form of cycles, just as day follows night in an endless succession of weeks, months and centuries. Even though day follows night, each day may differ from the previous, or following day. The actual substance of the Tao is the 'Chi', or 'material principle' of the force. Just as the chi flows through the universe, so it flows through the human being.

The idea behind the soft system is the harnessing of this principle, controlling its generation and flow through the body so that it is available to assist the body perform martial art techniques and to remain healthy. There are many stories of people who, suffering from terminal illness, have taken up a soft martial art like Tai Chi Chuan and apparently recovered from their complaint!

The ideal introduction to the soft systems is the style known as 'Hsing I', or 'Mind/Form Boxing'. The peculiar name comes from the concept which takes the principle of a movement, such as that of an animal and by using intuition and intelligence, produces a human movement which embodies the essentials. Thus in Hsing I there are many movements which are based upon animals and these are performed at speed but in a very relaxed manner.

An examination of some of the static stances used in Hsing I show that they closely resemble those used in the hard styles. The method of delivery, however, is different and there is no evidence of muscle spasms used to produce force. In demonstrations of Hsing I, students who are fairly advanced are able to show quite prodigious feats of breaking without apparent muscular effort. One exponent has demonstrated breaking three normal house bricks, whilst the other broke two bricks that were resting flat on top of each other on the floor. Despite these demonstrations, students of the internal styles do not condition their limbs. There are five basic forms of Hsing I and these all include movements attributed to animals.

After practising Hsing I for a while, the student moves onto a style known as Pa Kua. This is the 'Eight Trigram' style and is based upon the 'I Ching', or 'Book of Changes' that has been used for generations to foretell the future. The main part of the underlying theory involves the yin and yang symbolism which states that nature has two forces which are interrelated yet separate. The circling movements of the arms at the commencement of Pa Kua may very well represent this circular

In this Tai Chi sequence three separate blocks are concluded with a punch. The movements are very relaxed, and in real life are not performed slowly

view of nature and one is tempted to wonder whether there is any carry over from this into Karate, where some of the katas start with the arms describing a wide circle.

During Pa Kua training, the student walks quickly around the outside of an imaginary circle, in the centre of which is his opponent. He is seen to move his arms about vigorously and a close study reveals him to be performing a series of blocks, counters, evasions and strikes. At irregular intervals, he suddenly reverses direction.

It is very difficult to see how Pa Kua can be an effective fighting system, since the constant circling allows someone with anticipation to know where the opponent is going to be in the next few seconds. Someone who refused to stay still would cause the student of Hsing I to move in a series of ellipses, rather than circles. It is interesting to guess what effect this might have on his chi!

The most interesting of the three soft systems is 'Tai Chi Chuan', or 'Great Ultimate Fist'. Unlike the other two, this is performed slowly and people practising it seem to wave gracefully back and fore, rather like seaweed in the current.

Younger members of the hard schools scornfully deride it as the 'Old Man's Martial Art'; something that is practised once age prevents the more violent movements of youth.

Tai Chi Chuan is extremely popular all over the world, being seen primarily as a means of developing fitness and keeping supple. The repetition of its long form induces relaxation and a sense of peace, which must be cultivated if the inner secrets of the art are to be learned. An analysis of the dreamy, dance-like movements reveals a slow-motion series of valid martial art moves. A punch is evaded with a backward lean of the body and at the same time, a follow-up punch to the face is deflected as the body flows forward, sweeping away the opponent's feet, or pushing him bodily off balance.

The latter exercise, called 'Uprooting', is quite interesting. The practice of Tai Chi Chuan is supposed to let the chi sink to the feet, where it renders the exponent immovable. Not so the unfortunate partner, who is hurled upwards and backwards, often over unlikely distances. Yet another interesting demonstration has the students attempting to push the master over by

In Tai Chi Chuan, the moves are performed slowly and without muscle spasm

means of brute force. In some cases, the master will stand on one leg and still the students are unable to push him over! Some of these displays have, however, been demonstrated by persons who do not accept the existence of the chi. One such is Jean Allard, a physiologist with an interest in martial arts.

Allard is able to reproduce the demonstration of uprooting, by using simple leverage whilst pushing up and out. He also demonstrates how it is possible to prevent being pushed over by simply triangulating the force being applied, so that it acts against itself. His speciality, though, is reproducing the tremendous backwards flying leap of the person who has seemingly been but touched by the master. To achieve this, Allard stimulates a normal reflex action which is uncontrollably generated when the right stimulus is applied. Just as the bent leg jerks uncontrollably when the knee is struck, so the arms and legs fly forward when the pectoral muscle is stimulated by a sharp rap to the chest.

During the course of his fascinating work, Allard has discovered quite a number of points which, if struck, would produce unconsciousness or even death. An extension of his work shows how Tai Chi masters block with such great force yet without using obvious effort. This is because the block is made with a forward bent wrist and when the fingers contact the incoming technique, a relaxed snapping in of the palm can cause an extraordinarily strong deflection.

The concept of defeating strength through yielding is covered in other chapters but it does seem as though much of the original thinking on the subject originated in China. Suffice it to say that the same principles apply in Chinese martial art, where the opponent's energy is harmonised with and subsequently deflected or countered. In Tai Chi Chuan, for instance, the student is advised to use no more than a few ounces of muscle effort to defeat a ferocious attack!

Ceremonial Chinese spears

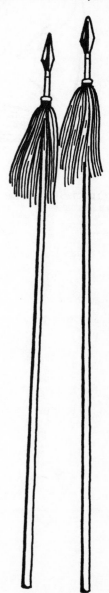

Another feature of Tai Chi Chuan training is called 'pushing hands'. To practise this, the one student will aim a technique at the other, whereupon the defender intercepts and guides it away from the target. During practice, a fair degree of effort is put in. Another training routine is called 'sticky hands' and this involves the one student laying his hand upon another's and then following its various movements. This type of training is also found in certain hard schools and is there to allow the opponent the opportunity of trying to sense when his partner is about to launch an attack.

Both hard and soft systems are similar in that they use what are called 'concurrent techniques'. These are when several moves are performed together. The body will move to one side to avoid a strike and simultaneously launch a counter-strike with one hand, whilst guarding the face with the other. These simultaneous movements contrast quite sharply with the serial, non-concurrent movements found in Karate and Taekwondo. Another similarity is that both Chinese systems include very short-range techniques that are extremely difficult to block. There is a disadvantage in having to draw back a fist, so as to give it enough distance to accelerate into a target. It is far better to be able to use a hand close to the opponent to deliver a telling blow. With no prior pull-back to warn, there is less chance of stopping the strike. A further advantage of short-range strikes is that they can be employed in any situation, such as in a car, or a telephone booth – where a longer punch doesn't have the space to build up force.

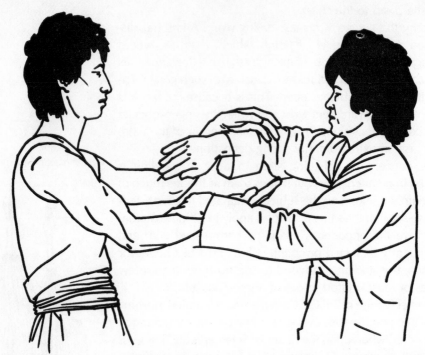

Both partners test the other for a weakness

Both systems use a lot of open hand techniques, whereas these have been largely replaced by the closed fist in Japanese practice. The open hand is a particularly useful weapon for accurate strikes to vital areas. Many Chinese systems follow the lines of the chi and will deliver a blow exactly on a meridian, causing immediate effect. Sometimes the effect of the blow does not wear off without some form of remedial massage – usually by the person who administered the blow. So potent are these strikes, that experts have knocked over a horse, merely by jabbing it with one finger on the right point!

It would be wrong to think of the Chinese martial arts as being unarmed. Weapons form part of the syllabus for almost every school. The famous Hunan warrior monks did not defeat their enemies with bare hands! The weapons on the battlefield were spears, halberds, broadswords, axes and bows. The Chinese bow is not used in current practice but the action of drawing a bow can be clearly seen in some movements. The broadsword is used in classical forms and in some cases two swords are used with the exponent leaping and spinning in a bewildering display intended to fight off multiple attackers.

The trident, halberd and spear also appear in forms, with the quarterstaff used both as a body conditioner and as a component of Shaolin forms. Other forms feature two short,

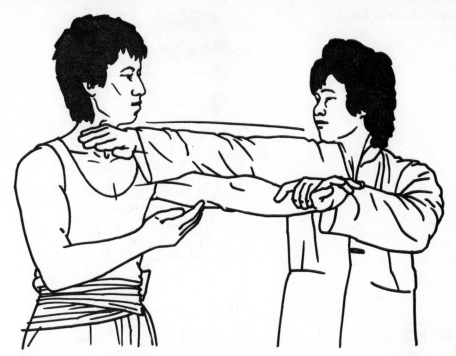

broad-bladed swords which are known as 'butterfly knives'. Others use short swords with a hook at the end, allowing them to be temporarily linked together and swung, like a composite weapon, through the air.

A momentary lack of concentration provides an opening which is immediately exploited

In addition to these, the Chinese developed a scientific form of wrestling called 'Shuai Chiao'. This art is traceable back to 500 BC when, together with archery, swordsmanship and horseriding, it formed part of the martial art training for the warrior. The original techniques were revised and improved through the years and in the sixteenth century an illustrated book of its techniques was circulated as far as Japan. The Japanese response to it was very swift and exponents of Shuai Chiao were invited to Japan in order to teach the techniques.

Shuai Chiao is practised from an upright posture and there are holds and throws but no sweeps, chokes, or ground work. Some of its techniques are almost indistinguishable from those used in Jiu Jitsu.

Kung Fu Today

Turning to the present time, the Chinese martial arts, now popularly known as 'Kung Fu', are the best known of all the arts through the film performances of Bruce Lee and the television series called 'Kung Fu'. Bruce Lee was an example of an innovator, initially trained in Wing Chun style Kung Fu

Butterfly knives are used in pairs

but who subsequently moved on outside its limits to study techniques of other styles. His own style was called 'Jeet Kune Do', or 'Way of the Intercepting Fist'.

A less respectable example of modern Kung Fu occurs in connection with the Chinese Triads. These are secret societies involved in criminal activities, such as gambling and drug smuggling. They originated from a much earlier secret society called the 'White Lotus' which functioned as an undercover political force and pressure group for six hundred years. This pressure group may have been originally set up with the assistance of the Shaolin warrior monks but its aims became other than religious during the ensuing generations. The Society underwent much splintering, especially following the communist takeover of the mainland. Some of its offshoots became associated with the already existing triads.

The triads contain one member, known as 'Red Pole'. He is the strong-arm man, or 'enforcer' of the group's will. Many of these are Kung Fu masters, though many Chinese teachers deny this, saying that they are merely killers. It is certainly a fact that one or two styles of Chinese martial art have become associated with the triads in recent years. One of these styles has achieved quite a degree of prominence through this dubious connection.

Because of the insularity of the Chinese, an overall governing body structure has been difficult to set up. The teachers will ask why they should join such a body and it is extremely difficult to provide an answer. Overall governing bodies are able to confer recognition but this is not sought by teachers who prefer to practise in obscurity. They are known by their reputations and serious students will seek them out regardless of whether there is official recognition. The true teacher of the Chinese martial arts does not favour large classes, because they do not lead to a proper student/teacher relationship. The question of finance is not altered by the size of the class, since an earnest student who wants above all to be taught by a certain master will pay the necessary amount.

Since most Chinese martial arts are not sports, then multi-school championships are rare. Where they do occur, there are great problems with the rules because of the diversity of methods used. With a punch that travels an inch or less, how is it possible to score it during hurried movements and from a distance? The answer can only be by allowing actual strikes to target areas, with attendant risk of injury.

The student who goes to a traditional Chinese martial arts club will find the atmosphere fairly casual in comparison with a Japanese dojo. There is much tea drinking during the lesson and an undercurrent of polite conversation. The master will often merely sit and watch the proceedings, whilst his senior students demonstrate and give advice. A new student is shown a technique to practise and is then left to get on with it for several lessons. From time to time, he will be watched closely to see if he is practising. No attempt is made to 'push' the student and it is left to him to decide whether he wishes to proceed or not.

When the beginner has developed a reasonable degree of skill at what he was originally taught, the senior student will offer some words of advice, or correct any small errors in performance. If the beginner is very lucky, the master himself may show an interest and make the odd comment. By this means, the beginner comes to learn more and more of the syllabus, until he has enough years of practice behind him to warrant the master's personal attention. From that time on, he becomes a senior student and is entrusted with the teaching of the beginners.

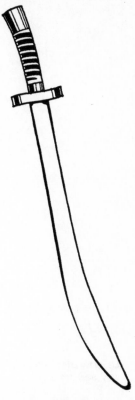

The Chinese broadsword is heavy and has a single cutting edge. It is held in a one handed grip

Using two rice flails requires very great dexterity

In classical Chinese martial art schools, there are no grades awarded. A student remains a student until released by the master to go out and open his own club. Because people have come to look for grades and coloured belts, they have been introduced into a great many schools which teach westerners and modern Chinese. The concept of a black belt, or 'sash' has been introduced, even though this is completely contrary to classical practice.

Another introduction to some schools has been the Nun-Chaku, or 'Rice Flail'. This weapon is described in detail under the chapter dealing with Kobudo. The rice flail originated in China and was used as a weapon by the peasants who were taught martial art by the Shaolin monks. Its practice had been all but forgotten until the Bruce Lee films created a cult interest that has not died away. The modern Chinese rice flail uses a bright steel chain to join the two batons. This is often slightly longer than in the Okinawan version, giving a longer effective range and a greater use as a garrotte. Several schools teach how to use a nun-chaku but usually the moves are of a showy nature, designed to promote coordination and timing, rather than for offensive purposes.

When considering using a rice flail, it is worth knowing that its possession in certain locations, including New York State can result in a police prosecution. If using a rice flail during training, students carrying it between the home and the club are strongly advised to wrap it in a towel placed at the bottom of the training bag. It is an even better idea to leave it at the club premises, if this is possible. The same comments apply to other traditional weapons.

Sparring sometimes takes place at the club, though often this is of a preplanned nature. The preplanned forms involve two or more people and can go on for a considerable time. Their object is to teach dangerous techniques with safety, yet in a manner approximating real fighting. During one such session, both students were armed with staffs and with one sweep the staff of one of the fighters caught and totally destroyed a solid wooden chair; for such is the power used during these practices! Other schools use padded jackets and mitts which allow the hand to be extended. The jackets are made of a canvas material strengthened with bamboo slats. Full power strikes are used to these, with no contact allowed to the head, groin or legs. One school has adopted a Karate-like style of semi-contact sparring, with heavy body contact, light head contact and no face contact. This style also allows the use of brightly coloured training tunics and succeeds in being an excellent spectator sport.

Other Chinese martial art clubs do not practise any sport aspect and prefer to concentrate on solid, self defence techniques. Techniques using weapons such as the fan and walking stick may be taught.

In Korea and Japan, both are used as part of certain self defence systems and one wonders whether these are in any way related to the Chinese techniques.

KOREA

1. THE CLASSIC ARTS

Hwarang-Do

There is a remarkable coincidence in the development of the early Korean martial art systems in that, like China, a Buddhist monk teaching from a temple in the mountains produced a long lived and major change in the development of martial art in that country. It is all the more surprising considering the time this training was alleged to have taken place – in, or around 540 AD. At this time, the Indian monk Bhodidharma was teaching in the Shaolin Temple and had already sparked off a sudden growth in that country's martial arts development.

The Korean 'Shaolin monk' was named Won Kwang and evidence does not confirm his nationality. Like the warrior monks of Shaolin, he was widely recognised as being the most skilled user of integrated martial arts. His reputation was such that he was invited to teach selected students of noble birth and others of known good character. This invitation came from King Chin Hung, the monarch of the Kingdom of Silla, in South East Korea. At that time, Silla was the smallest of the three kingdoms making up what is now the Korean peninsula.

The monk taught the young warriors, insisting that they not only be conversant with all the martial arts but be literary and religious too. This balance of ability was later to recur in other countries, such as Japan, where the Bushi were urged to become poets, philosophers and artists, in addition to their duties as warriors. The Korean code of ethics was also seen in other countries, its tenets being based upon loyalty, respect, obedience to one's superiors, integrity and perseverance.

The Korean warriors so trained came to be known as the 'Hwa Rang', or 'Flower of Youth' and their code of practice was referred to as 'Hwa Rang Do', or 'The Way of the Flower of Youth.' These young paragons served as the shock troops of the Silla period, overrunning and conquering the neighbouring kingdoms of Paekche in the South East and Koguryo in the North. Thus began Korea's first unification into a single country.

The three kingdoms of ancient Korea

An examination of the skills of the Hwa Rang shows a parallel development with Japan and China. The primary martial arts studied were those of horseriding, the spear, sword and the bow. In hand to hand combat, the Hwa Rang used the sword in a whirling, slashing pattern that can also be seen in Chinese forms. Korean swords were especially well made and the swordsmiths were much sought after by neighbouring nations.

The unarmed combat side was strictly of a secondary nature, being based upon grappling and throwing, rather than striking. In the training tournaments used to increase martial ardour, unarmed bouts were quite popular and the king became a patron. There is some evidence to suggest that wrestling was popular and a sport attracting royal patronage as far back as the fourth century. Tombs found near the ancient capital of Koguryo appear to show people engaged in some form of grappling.

The founders of some Korean martial arts have taken considerable licence when describing these arts as the forerunners of twentieth century systems! There is no doubt that the development of the grappling forms did play a part in the evolution of Korean martial arts but it appears that the major influence came from China (via the Shaolin Buddhist monks) and Japan.

It is said that the traditional martial art of Korea was called 'Soo Bahk Do' by the Hwa Rang and if so, then this may have been a fully integrated system, similar to the Wu Shu of China. With the dying out of traditional weapons in later centuries, the use of the sword became relegated to practice routines, based upon the old Hwa Rang systems. Vestiges of this sword-fighting are still seen in Korea today.

There are very few other examples of the art of the Hwa Rang because Korea was overrun by the Japanese in 1909. It remained occupied throughout the Second World War and its soldiers fought on the side of the Japanese. During this period of collaboration, the Japanese taught the Koreans Karate and Aikido. The Koreans absorbed these teachings, incorporating them with the older systems to produce the modern martial arts of Korea.

Hapkido

Hapkido is virtually Korean Aikido, with some elements of original Korean martial art included. The Hapkido symbol is written the same way as 'Aikido' but the Korean pronunciation turns it into 'Hapkido'. An examination of its basic principles reveals identical theories to Aikido, although phrased in a slightly different way. Hapkido describes itself as being based on three principles, which are:–

The principle of compliance, which is described as meaning the yielding to force, like still water that is penetrated by a thrown stone; offering no resistance and closing up immediately after the stone has passed.

The principle of deflection, which seeks to meet the attacker's force and by gentle guidance channels that force into a safe direction.

The principle of harmony, which calls for the attacker's force to be unopposed and harmonised with; so one's own force becomes added to that of the attacker's, rather than conflicting with it.

Exactly as in Aikido, the attacker is encouraged to over-commit, by way of a lunge, or a punch. The attack is received without any resistance; it is guided past the target and the defender's own force is added to it. The result of this is to unbalance and throw the attacker. Where there is no such commitment, the defender may allow the attacker to seize him, subsequently using a pressure point strike to weaken the hold. Once the hold has been weakened, it can be broken,

*Hapkido is a self defence art
sometimes incorporating
weapons*

using the principles of leverage and joint action. In many
cases, the Hapkido lock is applied against the joint movement, showing a close affinity with Aiki Jiu Jitsu.

Having broken the attacker's grip and placed him at a
disadvantage, a throw may be employed. These are extremely
like Aikido throws, relying upon the twisting of a joint such as
the wrist or elbow.

An examination of Hapkido strikes is interesting, showing
as it does some elements of Karate, Shaolin and the native
Korean kicks which are seen developed to such perfection in
Taekwondo. The Northern styles of Shaolin favour high kicks
and it is tempting to speculate that Won Kwang may have
come from, or been taught by, a Northern Shaolin Temple.

This is probably an absurd oversimplification, for parts of Silla, where the Hwa Rang trained, are quite hilly and this could have led to a preponderance of kicking techniques.

There are examples of high kicks and some quite spectacular jumping kicks that are obviously later additions – possibly from the same source as Taekwondo. Modern exponents of Hapkido also give breaking demonstrations, using wood and tiles to demonstrate the power generated. As an aside, it is curious to see the Korean preoccupation with breaking, or 'destruction' techniques. All three of the principal modern Korean systems indulge in some spectacular breaks and the only Karate style to do so is one devised by a Korean master.

Hapkido features all the common strikes, using the punch in the form common to Taekwondo users. The knife hand is used to strike and block and the extended single finger, or fingers, attack nerve points. Hapkido claims to have knowledge of some 300 vital points, teaching their use to selected high grade instructors.

The strikes of Hapkido are distinguished as being direct (front punch, front kick, side kick), or circular (knife hand strikes, turning kicks). The direct techniques cultivate the principles of 'snap action' – that of powering the technique out to the target, then abruptly withdrawing it so as to generate a whiplash action. The circular techniques tend to use the hips

Hapkido includes kicking as well as grappling techniques

and generate considerable power by means of body weight. Aikido type roll outs are also taught.

The incorporation of weapons into the syllabus shows that Hapkido may contain a much older element of integrated martial art. There are some advanced forms, taught only to black belts, which feature the broadsword. There is also a pattern performed with two curved short swords that may well be very ancient indeed.

The teaching of Hapkido involves a gradual change from hard techniques, to the soft, in much the same way as in China, the hard systems are generally held to come before the soft. In the basic practice of kicks and punches, the students first move in direct lines and are later introduced to the principles of evasion, culminating in the use of circular movements.

The tunic worn in Hapkido can vary from school to school. In some it is white, rather like a normal Taekwondo, or Karate suit whilst in others it is black, like that worn in certain styles of Chinese martial art. There are various grades of student progress called 'Kups' (equivalent to the kyu grades in Japanese styles) and the grades within the black belt are similarly known as 'Dans'.

In Korea, the governing body for Hapkido is a member of the Ministry for Sport. In previous years, it has been affiliated to the Ministry for Education. There are a number of different academies practising and each operates a different syllabus. Thus there are schools which stick closely with the original Aikido concept, as well as those which incorporate Taekwondo-like techniques.

Tang Soo Do

The Korean martial art of Tang Soo Do is something of a puzzle. Its founder, Hwang Kee, claims that its origins can be shown to go back some 2,000 years into Korean history, though he concedes that, in those days, it was known as 'Soo Bahk'. This is very similar to current claims made by the World Taekwondo Federation, who refer to the same cave drawings, sources of ancient manuscripts and sculptures as the Tang Soo Do people do. Obviously both cannot be right, and it is more likely that neither are!

The pictograms that make up the name 'Tang Soo Do' translate out as 'Way of the Tang Hand'. The similarity between this and the Okinawan pictograms for Karate cannot be ignored; they are identical. The related Korean martial art way of Kong Soo Do translates exactly as 'The Way of the Empty Hand'! The use of the word 'Do', or 'Way' is to be found a great deal in the Japanese systems and it relates to a peculiar change in the nature of a battlefield art, to one in which the development of the individual's character becomes of greater significance. This change is not common in China, where the Shaolin martial arts remained true to their effective and original forms.

To understand the arrival of the do forms in Japan, it must be realised that the government had restricted the opportunities of warfare and sought to have the troublesome warrior caste diverted by means of martial art 'Ways'. These do forms all followed the more practical 'jitsu' forms. On the other hand, the Koreans have arrived at the use of the analogous term 'do', for reasons which are not really clear. Moreover, they have described their martial arts (with the exception of Taekwondo) with exactly the same calligraphy as the Japanese arts and even gone so far as to adopt the same basic principles! In the case of Tang Soo Do, the resemblance is even more remarkable.

In defence of the claim that Tang Soo Do is largely based on ancient Korean martial arts, the Founder states that any similarities which are found between the Korean and Japanese systems are based upon the common, Chinese ancestry of both. To say that is akin to saying that because the wheel is the product of civilisation, it is reasonable to expect two countries, independently and simultaneously, to build a Model T Ford. The Japanese arts are quite different from the Chinese, though similarities can be traced if one compares old style Karate-jitsu with Southern Shaolin. On the other hand, the Korean styles (again with the exception of Taekwondo) so closely resemble the Japanese as to be almost indistinguishable.

Without doubt, the Japanese takeover of the Korean peninsula did much to damage the indigenous arts. At first, the people were not allowed to train in the arts but later, when Korean soldiers began to supplement the Japanese, it was considered a good thing to teach them Karate, Judo and Aikido. The practising of these arts had the same effect upon the Koreans, as it did on the Japanese – increasing their martial ardour and making them into more effective soldiers.

Because of the nearness of China and the existence of a definite indigenous art, the influence of the Japanese arts appears to have been variously modified. Circular techniques were in evidence and the peculiar interest in destruction techniques already established. With the end of the War, the Koreans may well have felt the need to identify their new found martial arts as clearly Korean, making them subtly different from that which had been taught. Thus the names were altered back to the original Chinese forms, with names like 'Chinto' replacing the Japanese name 'Gankaku'. Other Karate styles in Japan have also sought to return to their roots and have resurrected the name 'Chinto', plus a lot more – all of which are to be found in Tang Soo Do.

The student of Tang Soo Do will be expected to learn the five basic Hyung forms ('Heian katas' in Japanese) and it will come as no surprise to learn that they are virtually indistinguishable from the Japanese equivalent. The first time one attends a Tang Soo Do tournament and sees the forms competition, one could be forgiven for imagining it to be a Shotokan Karate event. Despite this astonishing resemblance, the founder of Tang Soo Do insists that these techniques are common to Korea, Japan and China.

In making these silly statements, Hwang Kee does much to detract from his own image, though fortunately without detracting from his own creation. It is no very bad thing to be similar to an excellent martial art way and Tang Soo Do is by no means an inferior system. In many ways, it surpasses the quality of its parent, particularly in the matter of kicks.

Tang Soo Do has cultivated the spectacular Korean kicks which are the envy of other systems. Not only are the classical straight kicks to be found but Tang Soo Do also uses the high circling and hooking kicks that did not appear in Karate until the 1970s. Thus, although a forms competition may be indistinguishable from Shotokan, the sparring looks nothing like it. If any parallels are to be drawn, Tang Soo Do sparring resembles the earlier forms of unarmoured Taekwondo.

The training tunic, or 'Tobok', is similar to that used in Taekwondo and there is a belt system of 'Kup' grades leading to the black belt, or 'Dan' grades. Training is in the form of lines and basic techniques are performed in the normal manner. From the basics of punches and kicks, the student is taken on to combination techniques, where individual basic techniques are linked together. There are also pre-arranged sparring bouts, where the attacker and defender alternate in role. Three step sparring is also practised, using the attacker to perform a series of three attacks. On the third, the defender uses a set defence. There is also free sparring and this allows light contact to be made.

A very praiseworthy habit of Tang Soo Do is the way its followers seek to integrate into the community like the old Chinese martial art 'sheriffs'. At grading times, when trainees are due for their next advancement in rank, a training hall is thoroughly cleaned out by the students. When clean enough, chairs are put out to accommodate the parents of students, the local police and any other dignitaries who express an interest. Several baskets of flowers make the occasion into a special one, rather than the 'conveyor belt', 'that'll be $20, thank you' of other schools. The Tang Soo Do student taking his grade feels that due importance is given to the result of all his efforts.

The other thing about Tang Soo Do is the close fraternity that forms between the clubs and the strong support that is given to the tournaments. Just as the exclamation 'Osu' is used in Nippon Kempo, so 'Tang Soo!' is used between Tang Soo Do members. This may be due to the very strong hierarchical structure that is found in Tang Soo Do, with the resident Chief Instructor having the final say on all technical matters.

In Korea, the Tang Soo Do Federation is organised into a governing body known as the Soo Bahk Do Hyup Hae. When the all-embracing concept of Taekwondo was suggested, the government asked the various Korean arts to amalgamate under it. The Tang Soo Do declined to do so, understandably not wishing to lose control of their clubs to another body.

2. TAEKWONDO - THE MODERN KOREAN ART

Just as baseball can be said to be the national pastime of the U.S.A., so Taekwondo is the national pasttime of South Korea. It is taught in schools, colleges and to the members of the armed services. Originally developed as a system of unarmed combat, it has also originated a form of competition so successfully that it is under consideration by the International Olympic Committee as a potential new game.

All of this has been achieved in a remarkably short space of time bearing in mind that the activity calling itself Taekwondo was only named as such in 1955! This is not to say that Korean martial arts did not exist before then but that was the year in which the name was first put forward. In a large number of Korean Taekwondo publications it has been falsely claimed that Taekwondo was practised many hundreds of years ago. One patriotic historian has attributed the development of Karate to an early Taekwondo influence whereas the reverse is most likely the case.

Students of Taekwondo must demonstrate the power of their attacks by means of destruction tests

Japan occupied Korea for many years and during the Second World War the two countries were co-belligerents. Many Koreans fought on the side of the Japanese and received

training in the Japanese martial art systems. This link comes across clearly in the case of 'Hapkido', the Korean reading of 'Aikido'. The extent to which the Japanese systems influenced the Korean cannot be gauged with certainty but from similarities in stance and technique, the influence in the formative years appears major. It is likely that the Japanese occupation led to the suppression and all but extinction of the native arts either by direct suppression, or by active encouragement of the Japanese alternatives.

Although the Koreans appear to have embraced these new systems, they did not entirely forsake their martial art heritage, with the result that all the Korean systems found today contain features which are clearly not Japanese influenced. Their infatuation with high and circling kicks is not a characteristic of the Japanese systems and it is likely that the Japanese actually learnt these from the Koreans. Since the rise in popularity of Taekwondo, Karate practitioners have adopted many of its techniques.

One of the most prominent personalities of Taekwondo is the originator of that name, Choi Hong Hi. Choi is a North Korean, who as a child was encouraged to study the old Korean techniques of Taekyun under the teacher Han II Dong. As a student studying in Japan, he learned Karate over a period of two years, eventually attaining the rank of first dan black belt. This combination of Korean and Japanese knowledge was to form the basis of his teachings at the academy of martial arts he founded in 1953. The name of the academy was the Ohdo Kwan, this translating as 'The School of my Way'. At the time, there were other academies in being and in the process of formation. All taught Japanese influenced systems. The names of these academies are still to be found in South Korea.

Being a professional soldier, Choi was able to introduce the teaching of his system to the men under his command. As time progressed, so he rose higher and higher and was eventually made general in the Korean Army. Through his military liaison with foreign units, Choi spread the knowledge of his system until it became international. In 1954 he became established as the Head of the Chongdo Kwan and sat on the board concerned with the development of a unified martial art development programme. His suggestion of the name Taekwondo (Hand/Foot Way) was enthusiastically received and applied as title for all the various Korean systems then practising.

Human nature being what it is, a number of academies preferred to retain their own identities and systems, rather than subordinate themselves to the Chongdo Kwan dominated 'Taekwondo'. As Choi's star continued to rise, he was appointed President of the Korean Taekwondo Association and organised the first international demonstration tour, the consequences of which contributed towards the eventual formation of the International Taekwondo Federation in 1966.

He succeeded in spreading Chongdo Kwan Taekwondo throughout South Korea, both in civilian and military life. In terms of military usage, the art was used in Vietnam as an integral part of the training in unarmed combat taught to certain units. It is thus very much a martial art and despite its title, not a martial art 'way'. Choi also promoted the sporting aspects of his school and his most spectacular success was in getting 'sport' Taekwondo accepted by the International Symposium of Military Sports.

In 1972, as a result of political pressure within South Korea,

Taekwondo uses a number of aerial kicks

Choi left the country to re-establish the headquarters of the International Taekwondo Federation in Canada. With his departure, the other academies of Korean martial art were released from the Chongdo Kwan influence and other developmental influences appeared. The Korean Taekwondo Federation quickly set up a rival international body to Choi's, calling it the 'World Taekwondo Federation'. In the year following Choi's departure, the World Federation held its first World Championships.

ITF Taekwondo fighters use full contact mitts and boots

Since that time, Taekwondo has been divided, with Korea encouraging the rapid development of WTF Taekwondo. This development shows several discontinuities – the earlier forms of patterns known as the 'Palgwes' were made obsolete and replaced by the 'Taigeuks' in a short space of time. Having seen WTF Taekwondo at the world headquarters in Korea not long after the setting up of the 'new' body, one could not help but notice the lower standard by comparison with ITF. It was obvious that Choi's Chongdo Kwan had taken advantage of his patronage to develop further and faster than the less favoured styles. Since then, however, the WTF has made tremendous strides in the improvement of standards and current comparisons show little difference at all.

Both forms favour the beautiful high kicks that are common

to the more ancient Korean forerunners. Both incorporate that uniquely Korean interest in wood and stone breaking as part of the actual syllabus. There is no doubt that the Koreans are masters of this particular art and it is curious that Karate, rather than Taekwondo, has become known for breaking.

For those who wish to see the most spectacular displays of breaking – or 'destruction' as it is more correctly known, then Taekwondo, is where to look. In the ITF competitions, there is a whole wealth of different events which include such things as 'power breaking', 'distance breaking' and 'height breaking'. In the first type, the object is to break as many one inch thick boards as possible with a technique such as a kick, punch, or open hand strike. The boards are held rigid in a wooden clamp standing on four legs. When using this clamp, accuracy is essential since injuries can occur when the technique inadvertently connects with the supporting struts of the clamp itself. It is for this reason that the WTF does not use the apparatus.

In the second type of destruction test, the competitors take a long run-up towards a line of polystyrene hurdles, throwing themselves forward and over the top. Whilst in the air, each competitor performs a flying side kick into the wood board target. The object in this type of competition is to cover as much distance in flight as possible. In the height test, the competitor jumps vertically and kicks straight upwards into the overhead horizontal target boards. The object here is to break wood held as high as possible.

Demonstrations of an unusual nature are often seen, with some competitors throwing wood into the air and breaking it as it falls, whilst others break a board suspended by a single strand of thread – without breaking the thread.

Taekwondo Techniques

In comparing the two schools of Taekwondo, many similarities are found and there is a quite clear link with the basic stances and movements of Karate – particularly those of the Shotokan school. Both employ a ready stance, with the feet slightly apart and the fists clenched. Both also employ a forward stance from which front and reverse punches are launched. In other examples, the WTF variety shows a move away from lower stances – no doubt reflecting the commitment to fast and effective sporting techniques.

Both forms use a cat stance, with the front foot resting only lightly on the floor. The back stances are similar and both have the sole of the front foot resting flat. WTF make much use of a high stance with the weight evenly distributed between front and rear legs. The feet are turned as they would be if the person was normally walking forwards. This forms the basic platform for fast technique delivery. Both use a straddle stance, with ITF calling for the feet to be parallel whilst WTF has them diverging slightly. A high intermediate stance is common to both, as is a curious 'in between' stance that is used to lead up to kick whilst stepping forwards or backwards. ITF has a curious, sanchin like stance that is not found in WTF and the latter has a one legged stance that can be found in certain Karate katas and Chinese systems.

As in Karate, the front fist is much in evidence and it is formed in the same way with the fingers rolling in and the thumb locking them. Curiously, Choi criticises as incorrect a form of the front fist which has the index finger unfolded along the palm. This method is seen only in the earliest forms of Shotokan Karate. The Taekwondo front fist is delivered from a variety of stances and employs a screwing motion of the wrist during delivery. This motion is found in the Shotokan derived schools of Karate but seldom in Chinese Boxing, where it is regarded as weak. The two forms of Taekwondo both use uppercuts and body hooks – neither of which are common to Karate. The double punch is found in Karate – particularly in the kata 'Bassai' and the method of using it in the WTF school is indistinguishable therefrom. In the ITF form, the same punch is generally delivered from a different type of stance. On the other hand, the horizontal punch of ITF is virtually identical to that used in the Karate kata 'Tekki'.

In the actual punch delivery system, the ITF form uses the Karate 'pull back' of the front arm to power the rear fist but it also calls for a drop into the final stance during punch delivery. The effect of this body drop is markedly to increase momentum. This up and down movement is not found in Karate, where appearance often counts for more than effectivity. ITF takes the analysis of power development very seriously and in knifehand, the hand is kept closed until the last instant, when the fingers fly out straight. This sudden spasm of action makes the strike much faster and therefore more powerful.

It is in kicking techniques that Taekwondo outstrips all other martial arts, with more different types than can be found anywhere else. An analysis of the ITF front kick shows a very interesting use of the hips to gain extra speed and snap. In most schools of Karate, the supporting leg swivels during the

A

B

C

D

In this sequence the opponent ducks under a snap punch and counters with a reverse punch. This twists the hips. The hip movement is translated into a reverse turning kick

development of the front kick and by this means, extra power and range result. In the Taekwondo front kick, the front foot remains forward pointing and both speed and power are generated by means of a forward hip thrust during delivery. Impact of this snapping kick is with the ball of the foot.

The turning kicks are all similar, using both the ball of the foot and the instep. When using the former, Taekwondo students are advised to impact with the leg as straight as possible whilst descending into the target. Thus when using a turning kick against the head, the foot must reach its maximum height just before impact, so that it drops slightly as it connects. This type of kick is very forceful but is more difficult to retract in the event of a sudden change in plans.

The reverse turning kick of Taekwondo has now been adopted in Karate, though the distinction between it and the similar reverse hooking kick has been lost in the transfer. To perform it, the kicker spins on the supporting leg, turning so that his back faces the opponent. Weight is taken on the front leg and what previously was the rear leg lifts off and straightens out. The continuing reverse turn of the body takes the kicking heel through a widening circular path until it impacts. In the case of a miss, the kick cannot be quickly retracted but the energy of the spin can be harnessed to a follow-up turning kick, or suchlike. In the case of the reverse hook kick, the attacker is assumed to be moving into the kicker. In this case, weight is transferred to the rear leg and the front lifts and hooks

E   F

with the heel to the back of the attacker's head. The reverse hook kick can also be performed using the defender's rear leg. In this case, the leg is brought quickly forwards, up and around to the back of the attacker's head.

More unusual kicks, not often seen outside Taekwondo, include the twisting kick. This is a snap kick which curves outwards during delivery. The impact area is the ball of the foot and the technique is useful when the opponent's body is angled, so that a direct front kick is not possible. The vertical kick resembles the crescent kick of Karate except that it tends to favour the outer edge of the foot rather than the inner edge.

A   B   C

For the jumping side kick, start from a high stance

Run forward and begin lifting the kicking leg

The body begins to turn in the air

This technique is useful for attacking a surface at right angles to the way the kicker is facing. A front thrust kick, using the heel/sole of the foot is often used in WTF sparring as a means of distancing the attacker prior to the defender loosing a second kick.

The side thrust kick is a strong Taekwondo technique, relying upon the swivel of the hips to drive the heel straight out and into the target. During delivery the supporting leg rotates away from the kick's direction and the body leans back. A guard is maintained during the kick. For the spectacular jumping side kick, a variety of opening moves may be made. The simplest involves a vertical jump, with the body rotating so that the kicking leg lashes out, heel forwards. The trailing leg is lifted as high as is practical.

This technique is performed to an opponent who is fairly close. With someone a little further away, the kicker can launch up and forwards, with the rear foot moving to the front as the body twists in flight. During the flying twist, the foot

D

The kick fully extends and impacts with the heel. The non-kicking leg is tucked up. The body is now fully side-on to the opponent

lashes out whilst the trailing leg is lifted high. The body leans back slightly and a strong guard is carried. For even greater distances, the short run-up is sometimes seen. In this technique, the body rises off the ground in a hips forward facing attitude and the rapid extension of the kicking leg pulls that hip forward behind it. With a little practice it becomes possible to do quite high kicks. With all jumping kicks, however, the landing is very important. This must be collected, so that if the kick has missed its target, the kicker is prepared to defend himself upon landing!

An even more difficult jumping technique is the jumping reverse turning kick. This requires a very agile reverse turn whilst airborne from a standing or running jump. The kick is powered by this twisting movement and the leg lashes out in a heel first circling motion. The angle of delivery for the kick is difficult to block effectively and evasion is the only effective counter.

The patterns show Karate-like movements but there is no

For the jumping/spinning reverse roundhouse kick, start from a high stance

Swivel so your back is facing the opponent

Spring clear of the floor whilst spinning

resemblance between Taekwondo patterns and Karate katas. Unlike Karate, the Taekwondo patterns are performed at uniform speed and there is no separation into fast blurs of movement separated by pauses. As a result of this, it is not so easy to visualise Taekwondo patterns as showing response to attacks from imaginary opponents; rather they are ways of getting students to associate techniques with as little thought as possible, so that in a conflict situation the defender can employ moves automatically and therefore quickly.

In ITF Taekwondo there are pre-arranged sparring sessions which differ from the WTF counterparts. The formal ITF pre-arranged sparring may involve more than one attack to which a deflection and counter is applied. In the WTF forms the scenarios are less rigid and there is a greater trend towards realism. As a result of this, the distinctions between pre-arranged and semi-free sparring begin to blur.

There is a little known section to ITF Taekwondo which deals with throwing and falling techniques. This section represents a selection of techniques which are quite different from the rest of the syllabus. A study of them reveals that they are very similar to the Shuai Chiao of the Chinese. There is no ground work and the throws are quite primitive by com-

Extend the kicking leg so that it sweeps around, the side of the foot arcing towards the opponent

D

parison with Judo. The moves may well have some relation to the older Korean arts. They form what is evidently a self defence part of Taekwondo training though it is fair to point out that for normal people they are unlikely to work.

In competition the two are quite different in concept. Choi's Taekwondo favours a non-contact regime, with reliance placed upon full contact boots and gloves to mitigate any inadvertent impacts. Choi opposes the use of armour since he theorises that all areas of the head and body are legitimate targets and therefore an overall armour would be required. By stopping the techniques short of actual impact, he is able to allow more realistic targetting. WTF, on the other hand, does not agree with the shadow boxing principles of ITF and calls for a system in which full contact attacks may be made to scheduled targets.

In order to be able to compete in a WTF Taekwondo match, the athlete must be in good condition and able to withstand more than one round of continuous action. Unlike Karate, the WTF Taekwondo match uses four corner judges, each with a notepad upon which they record clear hits to the target areas. At the end of the match, the referee collects the scoresheets for summation and averaging.

Regardless of the type of Taekwondo competition, there is less interruption than with a Karate match, where the referee panel is always having to discuss whether a point has been scored or not. On the other hand, the absence of punctuating breaks between significant techniques means that the one runs on into the next without pause for applause. In the WTF system the competitors wear padded jackets, but such is the force of some impacts that they have failed to prevent damage to the internal organs of the body. Also, where the action is continuous, the audience soon loses track of who is leading and the bout's conclusion is always something of a mystery.

Padded jackets are used to protect the body during WTF sparring

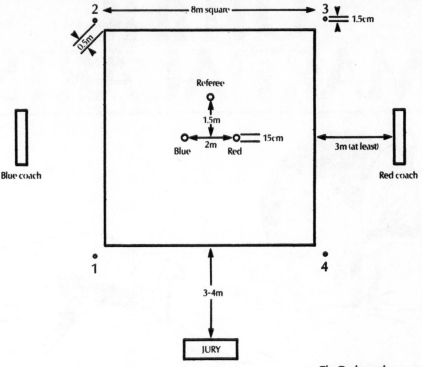

2 ← 8m square → 3 ↕ 1.5cm

0.5m

Referee
○
↕ 1.5m

Blue ○ ← 2m → ○ Red ▬ 15cm

↔ 3m (at least)

Blue coach

Red coach

1

4

↕ 3-4m

JURY

The Taekwondo competition area. The four judges' positions are marked on the area in white with a black numeral adjacent

Because of the full contact nature of WTF Taekwondo, there are no team matches as such and competitors are graded according to the following weight divisions:–

Under 48 Kilos (106 lbs.)	Fin Weight
Under 53 Kilos (117 lbs.)	Fly Weight
Under 58 Kilos (128 lbs.)	Bantam Weight
Under 63 Kilos (139 lbs.)	Feather Weight
Under 68 Kilos (150 lbs.)	Light Weight
Under 74 Kilos (163 lbs.)	Welter Weight
Under 80 Kilos (176 lbs.)	Middle Weight
Over 80 Kilos	Heavy Weight

In Junior categories, there are correspondingly lighter weight divisions. Both ITF and WTF tournaments include a women's sparring section but only ITF has a forms competition. The latter is held in both individual and team categories.

The World Taekwondo Federation is by far the larger of the two organisations. It has obtained recognition by the General Assembly of International Sporting Federations and is also accepted on to the International Olympic Committee. On the other hand, the ITF has secured recognition in a number of socialist countries not allied to South Korea's regime.

OTHER MARTIAL ARTS

1. FULL CONTACT

In America during the seventies, a need was felt to allow the widely different forms of martial art/combat sport to compete on equal terms. In that country, there were many large, mixed martial art tournaments, where exponents of Kung Fu competed against Taekwondo and Karate fighters. Now it is difficult enough to accommodate all the various styles of one system inside one set of rules for competition but it is quite another thing again to produce rules that will take in the characteristics of all the various combat systems.

Some styles of Kung Fu use very short movements and during a non-contact round, it is almost impossible to recognise potential scores in the welter of arms and legs. Therefore at an early stage American organisers decided that Full Contact was the only answer to the problem. Instead of estimating the effectiveness of a technique if it were to be allowed to land, the Full Contact technique would assess itself! The object in the match became that of knocking the opponent unconscious, or achieving a points lead at the end of the match.

Like boxing, Full Contact uses several rounds of competition and the professional contests take place in a boxing ring. With amateur fighters, the matches are held on open matted areas. The fighters wear brightly coloured long trousers with elastic waistbands. Normally a jacket or teeshirt is not worn. The fists are protected with boxing gloves or Full Contact mitts and the feet with Full Contact boots. The mitts are similar to boxing gloves but they have no palm to them – the fingertips being held by a band of material. The boots are of a sole-less design, with padded plastic covering the instep, side of foot and heel. The effect of these devices is to reduce the immediately damaging effect of the blow by spreading it over a wide area. Continuing blows to the head in Full Contact, as in boxing, lead to brain damage but the effects of this are not so immediately obvious as a bloody nose.

Because of the padding, the techniques used in Full Contact

*The Full Contact fighter
uses special gloves and
boots to mitigate impact*

changed and became more like boxing with kicks attached. For this reason, Full Contact is sometimes referred to as 'Kick Boxing'. An alternative name for it is 'Contact Karate', though this is a misnomer since activities other than Karate are involved. In many ways, the competition is similar to Thai Boxing and not infrequently one does see matches between Thai Boxers and Full Contact fighters. The Thai Boxers are, of course, not allowed to use their elbows and knees – otherwise the method of fighting is the same.

By moving completely away from the use of a concentrated technique to a weak area, Full Contact has moved clearly into the realms of combat sport. Unlike their colleagues in most traditional systems, Full Contact fighters go in for a great deal of body conditioning, so as to be able to retain stamina over a longer period whilst being able to take punishment. For this reason, Full Contact training uses much roadwork and bag work. Whereas many traditional arts practise techniques against the air. Full Contact measures efficiency in how hard and for how long the bag can be struck. Shadow boxing at the empty air does have a role to play but it is only a part of the overall training. Whilst the traditional martial artist waits for the opening to deliver one crushing attack, the Full Contact fighter dances around the ring, always weaving and jabbing.

Because Full Contact is of American origin, the fighting weights are given in pounds. The kilogramme equivalent is given in brackets afterwards.

Below 125 lbs (56.8 kg)   Flyweight
Below 139 lbs (63.2 kg)   Super Flyweight
Below 152 lbs (69.1 kg)   Lightweight
Below 163 lbs (74.1 kg)   Welterweight
Below 173 lbs (78.6 kg)   Middleweight
Below 184 lbs (83.6 kg)   Light Heavyweight
Above 184 lbs (83.6 kg)   Heavyweight

There is no overall international governing body for Full Contact and consequently there are a number of 'World Champions'. The two major international bodies are the 'Professional Karate Association' and the 'World All Styles Combat Organisation'. Only comparatively recently have national governing bodies been set up in some countries. Previously, the sport formed a fringe activity of many of the traditional systems. The inducement to set up a governing body is twofold. In the first case, the fighters' health must be safeguarded and this means a central registry. The registry keeps competition details which allow the fighter to be 'rated' on past performance. By means of this, fighters of comparable abilities are matched and there is little chance of one getting badly beaten. The registry also records when a fighter has been knocked out. Following a knock out, a fighter may not compete for a specified period of time because doctors have found out that the effects of brain damage increase when there

*The object in Full Contact is
to knock out, or gain a
points advantage over the
opponent*

are several injuries sustained in a short period. Therefore
every fighter must be rested after head injury.

Previously, it was possible for a fighter to get knocked out in
one match on Saturday, then to travel to another part of the
country on the Sunday and fight again. To prevent this, Full
Contact fighters carry with them a personal record in the form
of a registration book. This must be shown to the match
organisers before anyone is allowed to get into the ring. Every
time a fighter is injured, his personal record is endorsed and a
card is also sent to the central registry. To make it even more
safe, Full Contact fighters have to have an annual medical
which really goes into all aspects of their health. Each time
they go into the ring, their health is checked by the tournament doctor.

Because of the injury risk in Full Contact, the majority of
members do not compete. This does not stop them from
merely training, however, and syllabuses have been devised
which use a system of coloured belts, just like in traditional

schools. To progress, the student learns techniques in exactly the same way as he would in, say, a Karate school. To be sure, there is less reliance upon stance training and much more on the art of moving quickly in all directions. The techniques taught are very similar to those already discussed in other chapters. There are snap punches, reverse punches, straight kicks, turning kicks and even jumping kicks! Rather than the rigid performance of a technique such as a punch, the Full Contact athlete is encouraged to perform on the move and in conjunction always with a block, feint, or evasion. Because Full Contact is such an open sport, attracting Kung Fu, Taekwondo and Karate, the techniques it uses are taken from all three and whereas it may have once been possible to identify from which traditional art a particular fighter came, it is no longer possible to do so.

Full Contact training is popular because of its informal and flamboyant methods. The use of hand and foot protection allied to light contact practice sparring makes for extremely enjoyable training. Using a bag gives a real idea of effectiveness and moving target mitts generate accuracy. The training is very similar to that found in Free Style Karate, where punches and kicks are not locked out rigidly but rather flow together into a sequence. For the person who has not been attracted by the mystery, or Eastern theory behind the traditional systems, Full Contact provides a no-nonsense and practical form of physical training allied with an effective means of self defence.

2. OTHERS

Thai Boxing

Thai Boxing is one of the hardest of all the combat sports. Putting it under the banner 'martial art' serves for convenience rather than accuracy, since it has never been an art of war. It involves no practice of forms, or basic techniques and no pretence at improving the character. It is quite simply a superb fighting art which, in its native form, is surely the most deadly of all.

In Thailand, there are about eight hundred training camps in which Thai Boxing is taught. These camps are run by one time boxers for young hopefuls, taken on from the age of twelve. At first, the youngsters are made use of as servants and cleaners but after a while they are introduced to light work on the kicking bag. In the steamy heat of the Thai climate, the compounds have no need for walls and there is normally just a roof, a boxing ring and some bags.

The fighter must build up tremendous stamina to last the full distance, for the art is more strenuous than Western boxing. Bag work serves as the basis for power development and the fighter works to build up the suppleness needed to kick repeatedly high and hard. The weapons used are the fists, the elbows, the knees and the shin/instep. Boxing gloves protect the hands but there is no protection at all for the elbows, knees or feet. The elbows and fists are used against the head, whilst the knees are allowed to contact the ribs with full force. The feet are the most fearsome weapons, being used to attack any target from the thighs upwards!

Whereas the normal Karate or Taekwondo kick tends to flick out and back, the Thai turning kick to the head comes off a straight leg and if it misses, it continues on over! Despite the long action, the kicks are phenomenally fast and impact with the shin, rather than the instep. To use the knee, the Thai Boxer grabs his opponent's head and tries to drag it down. Alternatively, he may repeatedly strike the upper arms, so that they begin to sag, allowing an opening for a turning kick to the head.

Just as in Western boxing, there are intervals between rounds, when the fighters are fanned and otherwise ministered to. Accompanying the match, from beginning to end, is the music of Thai bagpipes, producing a wailing that seems to encourage them to get in and mix it. Every time there is an eruption of fighting, the music stops, only to start again during

The use of knee techniques is legitimate in Thai Boxing

the ensuing lull. It is curious to see the Thai boxers swaying faintly to the music as they square up. At the outset of the match, the boxers show their paces in the form of a ritual dance or 'Ram Muay'. A ritual headband, called the 'Mong-kon' is worn during the dance but it is removed for the fighting.

Each compound has a specific form of ritual dance, which calls upon any friendly spirits in the area to help them defeat their opponent. The movements in the dances are symbolic and can include pseudo threatening gestures made to the opponent.

Thai Boxing is regarded as the forerunner of the 'Boxe Francaise', or 'Savate' as it is sometimes called. For a long time, the French occupied parts of Indo-China and Count Pierre Barruzzy, the President of the French Federation has confirmed the connection.

Thai Boxing is not the only art of Thailand, there is another called 'Krabee Krabong'. A 'Krabee' is a knife or sword and a 'Krabong' a spear or staff. This art goes back into antiquity and is said to have been introduced by a Siamese king who wished to oppose Chinese domination. The system uses a wicker shield and a short sword or spear. In some cases, if no shield is used, then two swords are employed to produce a continual rain of cuts.

The swords are slightly curved, with blades that broaden towards the tip. They have a single cutting edge and the blade is weighted to give a better cut. The handles are long and wooden, with only a small finger guard. They are perfectly round in section and may have some form of ornamental ribs spaced out along their length. The shield is round and is composed of concentric rings of woven fibre.

To practice with the weapons requires many years of effort and all routines involving them are carefully worked out, so that they are in effect, pre-arranged forms. In use the swords are deployed with a slashing action, the shield and other sword being used to fend off counter-attacks. Interestingly, there are also kicks and trips used though these are rather hurriedly performed to avoid the possibility of having a leg chopped off!

Viet Vo Dao

'Viet Vo Dao' means 'The Way of Vietnamese Martial Art'. As its name implies, it encompasses a great many individual arts, including both weapon and weaponless systems. It seems likely that Viet Vo Dao was a true military art in view of the highly effective forms that use the sword, the butterfly knives, the short staff, the rice flail and the halberd. The last great master of the system was Nguen Loc and in 1938 he collected all the separate elements and brought them together under one title.

In the years since the collapse of Vietnam, the arts have been maintained and are practised in the countries where the Vietnamese have found new homes. France is the main centre for Viet Vo Dao, having the highest population of Vietnamese through its previous territories in Indo-China.

Loc believed that the study of the martial arts would encourage the ideal of fraternity between all races and creeds. It is for this purpose that he established the system.

Whilst the unarmed system in Viet Vo Dao is in many ways similar to Karate or Taekwondo, it also includes some quite spectacular grappling techniques, not the least of which are the 'jumping scissors'. In this technique, the attacker jumps clear off the ground and wraps his legs around the opponent's neck, stomach, or knees. When used against the neck, a twisting movement of the legs causes fracture and instantaneous death.

There are forms to be practised, just as in Karate, and they are known as 'Quyen'. In order to separate them, they are referred to as numbers one, two, three etc. The practice tunics are black in colour but otherwise similar to that worn in Karate. A coloured belt system operates, with elementary grades leading to the black belt.

Mersilat

'Mersilat', or 'Bersilat' merely means, 'To do Silat', the latter being the name given to the martial art system of Malaysia. Over the years, Malaysia has been invaded by countries such as Thailand and China so it comes as no surprise to see evidence of foreign systems incorporated within it. In the last seventy years, Judo and Karate techniques have also been introduced so that Silat emerges as a very mixed bag indeed!

The original Silat is believed to have originated in the fifteenth century and since then, it has been firmly linked with the practice of the Islamic religion. The art is widely spread throughout Malaysia, being practised in the villages, or Kampongs. It is customary to see demonstrations of it at weddings and civil celebrations, where it is put on to the accompaniment of music.

In the cities, the teaching of Silat is often of poor quality and the art is adulterated with others. In the kampongs, however, it is still possible to see the original Silat, or 'Gayong' as it is referred to. Silat consists of both armed and unarmed systems, with striking and grappling techniques in the latter and the use of swords and knives in the former.

Silat is not practised as a sport and sparring tends to be pre-arranged. Typically, both fighters, whether armed or otherwise, will circle each other warily, searching for openings. The attack, when it comes, is hard pressed, with the attacker hoping to discover a weakness in the opponent's defence. In traditional Silat, there are no grades between student and master, though in the cities such modern practices have been introduced.

Escrima

Escrima is an old Spanish word meaning 'skirmish'. It is also the name of a violent and effective system developed in the Philippines over five hundred years ago. Originally it was widely taught, under the name 'Kali', showing by this its relationship to the Sanskrit studied at that time. The system is primarily an armed one using the baton, machete, or dagger. Weapons may be used in pairs and latterly there has been a successful attempt to introduce Judo and Karate techniques into the repertoire.

When the Spanish invaded the Philippines in 1521, they learned first hand the effectiveness of the system and when their rule had been secured the natives were forbidden to

Escrima sticks may be used singly or in pairs

carry arms, or practice 'Arnis de Mano' (Art of the Hand) as the Spaniards called it. As a result of this ruling, the art was driven underground and functioned secretly until the Spaniards were replaced by the Americans in 1889. The Americans struck up a good relationship with the Philippinos and found them willing allies in the Second World War. Army issue machetes were much appreciated by the natives and used extensively during guerilla operations.

The art of Escrima is combat oriented, with frequent championships and competitions. The contestants circle and hack violently at each other, holding the batons a hand's width from the end. The butt end is particularly useful for short range clubbing techniques and trapping the opponent's baton.

Beginners are taught by taking them through a sequence of repeating techniques, using two batons. These techniques are mirrored by the opponent, with the result that they clash with each move. Both partners move simultaneously and as soon as the rhythm is built up, some quite fast moves result. As the pair become more expert, body leans and steps are employed, all incidental to the basic rhythm of stick movement.

A pair of Escrima sticks

GLOSSARY

Explanation of Glossary
The words in brackets refer to the country of origin, such that:—

JP	=	Japan
CHI	=	China
KO	=	Korea
ML	=	Malaysia
FR	=	France
THAI	=	Thailand
SP	=	Spain
PHIL	=	Philippines

AIKI (JP) Harmony with life force.

AIKIDO (JP) Martial art way meaning 'Way of all Harmony'.

AIKI JIU JITSU (JP) Martial art predecessor of Aikido. Means 'Compliant and Harmonious Techniques'.

ARMLOCK A hold which twists, locks, or overextends a joint of the arm.

ARNIS DE MANO (SP) Philippine martial art using sticks or knives. Means 'Hand Art'. See also 'Escrima'.

ART Any specific skill. Martial arts are the arts of war – 'The Battlefield Arts'. Japanese term is 'Jitsu'.

ATEMI (JP) Striking to the vulnerable areas of the opponent's body.

AXE KICK A downwards travelling kick which impacts with the heel.

BACK FIST A punch made with the back of the two large knuckles.

BACK KICK Kick which travels directly backwards and impacts with the heel.

BACK STANCE Stance in which the majority of body weight is taken on the rear foot. The front foot may lie flat, or the heel may be raised from the floor.

BALL OF FOOT Pad of flesh at base of the toes. When toes are pulled back, the ball of foot is used as an impact area in kicks.

BASICS Fundamental techniques from which combination techniques and forms are built up.

BASSAI (JP) A Karate kata of the Shuri-te School. Several different forms exist and there are two different katas under the name 'Bassai' – 'Sho' and 'Dai'.

BELT Sash worn around the waist of the training tunic and often coloured to show state of progress. Black belt is mark of highest achievement.

BERSILAT (ML) Malaysian term meaning 'To do Silat'. See also 'Mersilat' and 'Silat'.

BHODIDHARMA See 'Daruma'.

BLACK BELT Sash worn around waist which is black in colour. Denotes high achievement. See also 'Dan'.

BO (JP) A quarterstaff used by Japanese and Okinawans for combat purposes.

BOGU (JP) Armour worn in Japanese styles.

BO-JITSU (JP) Techniques involving use of a Bo.

BOKKEN (JP) An imitation Japanese sword carved from heavy wood.

BOW To bend the head forwards. A form of greeting used in the martial arts and ways.

BOXING, CHINESE System of Chinese combat. May be hard as in Shaolin, or soft as in Tai Chi Chuan. See also Chuan Fa, Kung Fu and Wu Shu.

BREAKFALL Way of falling safely, where the arm strikes down on the mat to reduce body impact.

BREAKING Also known as 'Destruction'. The practice of breaking wood, tiles, or stone in order to demonstrate the force of techniques.

BROADSWORD A curved, single edged heavy sword used in Wu Shu practice.

BU (JP) 'Military', or 'Martial'. Used with other words as in 'Bu Jitsu', which means 'Military Techniques'.

BUDDHISM Far Eastern religion which spread from India to China, Japan and Korea. Appears implicated in the development of the martial arts in those countries. See also 'Zen' and 'Chan'.

BUDO (JP) Means 'Military Ways', a code of behaviour which seeks to improve the character of the person studying it.

BU JITSU (JP) See 'Bu'.

BUSHI (JP) High ranking Japanese warrior, often of noble birth.

BUTTERFLY KNIFE Short, broadsword-like knife with hand guard. Used in pairs for practice of some styles of Chinese martial art and Viet Vo Dao.

CAT STANCE Basic stance in which virtually all the body weight is on the rear foot, with the front foot merely touching the floor.

CHAN (CHI) The Chinese reading of 'Zen'.

CHI (CHI) Material principle of energy. See also 'Ki' and 'Internal Power'.

CHINTO Name of Chinese military attaché to Okinawa. May have originated kata named after him. Chinto is also the name of a kata of the Shuri-Te school.

CHOY (CHI) One of the 'Five Ancestors' of Shaolin martial art.

CHUAN FA (CHI) 'Fist Way', the term used to denote Chinese Boxing. See also 'Chuan Shu'.

CHUAN SHU (CHI) Another term meaning Chinese Boxing.

CIRCULAR BLOCK A way of blocking a technique by means of a circular arm movement. Found in Kyokushinkai Karate and Taekwondo.

CLAW HAND Open handed attack with fingers crooked.

COMBINATION TECHNIQUES A series of basic techniques performed consecutively.

CONTROL Regulation of force used in performing a technique so as to avoid injuring the opponent.

COUNTER A retaliatory move made to an attack.

CRANE A school of Chinese martial art which bases its techniques upon the movements of the crane.

CRESCENT KICK A turning kick with the toes pointing upwards. The curled inside edge of the foot is used to deflect the opponent's arm, or to strike at the face.

DAN (JP & KO) Stage within the black belt. First Dan,

Second Dan etc., to maximum of Tenth Dan.

DARUMA (JP) The Japanese name for the Indian monk Bhodidharma (known also as 'Ta Mo' in China). Allegedly the person who introduced Zen (Chan) Buddhism to China and initiated the systematic study of the Chinese martial arts at the Shaolin Temple.

DEFENCE Move made to safeguard oneself.

DO (JP & KO) Used at the end of a name, such as Karate-do and meaning 'The Way of'. Arts which use 'do' are those which seek to improve character of those studying them.

DO (JP) Mid-body protector.

DOJO (JP) 'Place of the Way'; the training hall used for the practice of Japanese martial art.

DRUNKEN FORM A form in Chinese martial art in which practitioners move as though drunk.

EDGE OF FOOT The outer edge of the foot which follows the heel into the target when used in side kick.

ELBOW Close quarter weapon used against opponent's chin, or mid section.

EMPTY HAND The meaning of 'Karate'.

ESCRIMA (SP) See 'Arnis De Mano'. This Spanish expression means 'Skirmish'.

EXTERNAL SYSTEM A system of Chinese martial art which uses muscle power in the execution of techniques. Also known as a 'Hard System'.

FIST Area of hand used in many punching techniques. There are many varieties of fist, including front fist, back fist and hammer fist.

FIVE ANCESTORS The five survivors of the Shaolin Temple who gave rise to five main lines of Shaolin development.

FLYING KICKS Any type of kick in which both feet are clear of the ground during impact.

FOCUS The concentration of power at one particular point in the delivery of a technique.

FORM A pre-arranged series of techniques based upon a response to imaginary attackers. Also known as 'Kata', or 'Pattern'.

FORWARD STANCE A stance found in Karate where the hips are rotated forwards, the front leg is bent, with the knee directly above the instep. The rear leg is straight.

FREE FIGHTING See 'Free Sparring'.

FREE SPARRING Where opponents engage each other in unprogrammed combat.

FRONT KICK A kick delivered with the ball of the foot, in which the kicking knee rises vertically.

FULL CONTACT Combat in which full power kicks and punches are delivered. Contestants use padded boots and boxing gloves.

GI (JP) Training tunic worn in Japanese martial arts, 'Karate-gi', 'Judo-gi'.

GOHO (JP) The 'hard' system of Shorinji Kempo.

GOJU RYU (JP) Style of Karate, originated in Okinawa by Chojun Miyagi.

GRADINGS An examination of the competence of a student to see whether advancement is in order.

GRAPPLING TECHNIQUES Those martial art moves which involve seizing, holding, throwing and joint-locking techniques.

GUARD The position of the hands and legs relative to each other.

GUNG FU (CHI) A pronounciation of 'Kung Fu'; a common name for the Chinese martial arts.

HAKAMA (JP) The split skirt garment worn in some Japanese systems.

HAKKO RYU (JP) One of the schools of Jiu Jitsu.

HALBERD A spear like weapon mounted on a long staff and with an auxiliary cutting edge below the point. 'Helmet Breaker.'

HAMMER FIST The little finger side of the closed fist, used like a club.

HAND CONDITIONING The process of making the hands less sensitive to pain, usually by damaging the skin and bones so that they respond by building up callus.

HAPKIDO (KO) A Korean martial art meaning 'The Way of Harmony'. Very similar to Aikido but with an expanded syllabus that includes kicks and hand strikes.

HARD SYSTEM Term used in Chinese martial art. See 'External System'.

HEEL KICK Any kick which uses the heel as the impact area.

HEIAN (JP) The name given to a class of five basic Karate katas in Japan. Also known as 'Pinans' in some Karate schools.

HIDDEN MOVES Those techniques sometimes found in a Karate kata which have no apparent meaning.

HIPS The part of the body most frequently used to provide power for punches and kicks in some Japanese and Korean systems.

HONBU (JP) The headquarters for any particular Japanese martial art.

HORSE STANCE Another term used to describe the straddle stance found in some martial arts.

HSING I (CHI) A soft style of Chinese martial art which bases some of its techniques upon the actions of animals.

HUNG GAR (CHI) One of the Five Ancestor Styles of the Shaolin Temple.

HWA RANG (KO) A warrior caste raised during the Silla Dynasty of Korea.

HWA RANG DO (KO) The code of ethics used by the Hwa Rang.

HYUNG (KO) A series of Tang Soo Do basic katas (forms, or patterns) which are analogous to the Heians of Karate.

IAIDO (JP) The Japanese martial art way of drawing, deploying and returning the sword.

IAI JITSU (JP) The practical techniques of sword drawing, deploying and re-sheathing.

I CHING (CHI) An ancient book which describes methods of foretelling the future.

INSTEP Part of the foot used in the execution of kicks such as the groin kick.

INTERNAL POWER The energy that is derived from 'Chi'. See also 'Ki'.

INTERNAL SYSTEM A system of Chinese martial art which relies upon the use of internal energy or 'Chi'. See also 'Soft System'.

ISHIN RYU (JP) A school of Karate based on a fusion of Wado Ryu and Kyokushinkai. The founder is David Donovan (GB).

ISSHIN RYU (JP) A school of Karate based on several Okinawan schools. The founder is Tatsuo Shimabuku.

IPPON (JP) A decisive point scored in a Japanese martial art way competition.

JEET KUNE DO (CHI) Name given by Bruce Lee to his personal fighting system.

JION (JP) A Karate kata belonging to the Tomari-te school of Okinawa.

JIU JITSU (JP) A Japanese martial art based upon the use of 'compliance' in using an opponent's strength against him.

JITSU (JP) See 'Jutsu'.

JIYU IPPON KUMITE (JP) A form of pre-arranged sparring which is near to Free Fighting.

JO (JP) A short staff measuring about 130 cms in length.

JODO (JP) The Japanese martial art way of using a Jo.

JO JITSU (JP) Practical techniques using the Jo.

JU (JP) The principle of yielding, or giving way.

JUDO (JP) The 'Compliant Way', a Japanese system where the opponent's strength is used to his disadvantage. School of refined Jiu Jitsu founded by Jigoro Kano.

JUDOKA (JP) Person who practises Judo.

JUHO (JP) The 'soft' system used in Shorinji Kempo.

JUTSU (JP) A Japanese term which means 'Techniques'. It refers to practical methods which are based on effectivity.

KALI (PHIL) The forerunner of 'Arnis de Mano', the Philippino art of stick, or knife fighting. See also 'Escrima'.

KAMA (JP) The sickle which was used by Okinawan Karateka in their fighting system.

KANKU (JP) A Karate kata also known as 'Ku Shanku'.

KARATE (JP) A Japanese martial art, using strikes and kicks. The Okinawan predecessor also includes weapon techniques. Depending on how it is written in Japanese, 'Karate' can mean 'Empty Hand', or 'Hand of China'.

KARATE-DO (JP) 'The Way of the Empty Hand', a Japanese martial arts way.

KARATE-GI (JP) See 'Gi'.

KARATE-JITSU (JP) The effective techniques of Karate.

KARATEKA (JP) Person who studies Karate.

KATA (JP) See also 'Form' and 'Pattern'. A stylised self defence against imaginary attackers; often quite long and involved and sometimes including 'hidden moves'.

KEMPO (JP) A Japanese system of striking or kicking with a possible Chinese influence. 'Kempo' is the Japanese reading of 'Chuanfa'.

KENDO (JP) Japanese martial arts way based on the use of the bamboo shinai.

KENDOKA (JP) Someone who practises Kendo.

KENJITSU (JP) The techniques of using the sword in a practical sense. This martial art includes unarmed as well as armed combat techniques.

KI (JP) The name for inner power, or energy used in the execution of 'soft' techniques. See also 'Chi'.

KIAI (JP) The shout used by Japanese martial artists to concentrate their energies.

KICK BOXING Any combat sport which employs full contact techniques. This term is usually applied to Full Contact and Thai Boxing.

KICKS Use of the legs in striking techniques.

KIHON (JP) The basic training moves which are repeated many times in order to reach competence.

KNEE Part of the leg used in close range techniques.

KNIFE HAND Open hand striking and blocking technique, using the little finger edge of the hand as the impact area

KOBUDO (JP) The old martial art ways but specifically those involving weapons.

KODOKAN JUDO The name given by Kano to his refined school of Jiu Jitsu. Now an Olympic combat sport.

KOHAI (JP) Junior student.

KRABEE-KRABONG (THAI) Armed system of Thailand using swords and shields.

KUNG FU (CHI) The nonsense words that have come to be used to popularly describe the Chinese martial arts.

KUSARIGAMA (JP) A composite weapon consisting of a sickle to which is attached a length of light chain with a weight at the end.

KYOKUSHINKAI (JP) A Karate style founded by Masotatsu Oyama. The name means 'Way Of Ultimate Truth'.

KYU (JP) A grade of competence below black belt level, often denoted by a coloured belt.

KYUDO (JP) A martial art way meaning 'The Way Of The Bow', involving the study of correct form and posture and through this the improvement of the character.

KYU JITSU (JP) The martial art of archery.

LAI (CHI) One of the Five Ancestors styles of the Shaolin Temple.

LAU (CHI) One of the Five Ancestor Styles of the Shaolin Temple.

LOCK Technique which immobilises a joint.

MAKIWARA (JP) A striking post used to condition the hands and feet.

MARTIAL Pertaining to war; military.

MARTIAL ARTS The Military Arts; the Arts of War.

MEN (JP) The head and face protector used in Kendo and Nippon Kempo.

MERSILAT (ML) Malaysian fighting system.

MOK (CHI) One of the Five Ancestor styles of the Shaolin Temple.

MOKUSO (JP) Silent meditation practised often before or after training.

MONKEY STYLE A school of Chinese martial art with moves based upon the characteristics of the monkey.

MOODUKWAN (KO) An academy of martial arts practice.

MUAY THAI (THAI) The combat sport of Thai Boxing.

NAGINATA (JP) A form of spear with a sword-like cutting edge.

NAHA-TE (JP) One of the three original styles of Okinawan Karate.

NAI HANCHI (JP) A Karate kata from the Okinawan Shuri-te school.

NINJA (JP) 'Stealers In'. Mercenaries and specially trained soldiers used to infiltrate.

NINJITSU (JP) The techniques of the Ninja.

NIPPON KEMPO (JP) A combat sport based upon Karate, Judo and others founded by Sawayama.

NIPPON SHORINJI KEMPO (JP) The Japanese form of Shaolin Temple Boxing founded by Michiomi Nakano.

NORTHERN STYLES A group of Shaolin styles that developed in the North of China. They are characterised by kicking techniques and open stances.

NUNCHAKU (JP) The rice flail; two wooden batons linked by a universal joint.

OKINAWA TE (JP) 'Okinawa Hand', the collective term for the schools of Okinawan Karate. Also abbreviated to 'Te'.

ONE KNUCKLE PUNCH A punch in which the middle joint of the middle finger projects and is used as the impact point. Also known as 'Phoenix Eye Punch'.

ONE STEP SPARRING A form of pair practice in which a specific attack is countered in a specific way.

OSU (JP) A verbal expression of acknowledgement.

PA KUA (CHI) One of the internal forms of Chinese martial art. The movements are soft, relying upon inner power.

PALM HEEL The lower part of the palm, next to the wrist. Used to deliver a strike.

PARRY To redirect an opponent's attack.

PATTERN See 'Kata' and 'Form'.

PHOENIX EYE PUNCH See 'One Knuckle Punch'.

PINAN (JP) A set of five basic Karate katas originating from the Shuri-te school of Okinawan Karate.

POSTURE The alignment of the body at any point.

PRAYING MANTIS A school of Shaolin Temple Boxing.

PREARRANGED SPARRING A method of practice in which the attacks and defences are arranged beforehand.

PRESSURE POINT A point on the body which, when pressed, causes pain, unconsciousness, injury or death.

RANDORI (JP) A form of Free Sparring, where techniques are not prearranged.

RANGE The distance between opponents.

RANK The position of a martial art student in the ladder of progression for that art.

READY STANCE A relaxed stance, from which a positive move can be made.

RECOIL The force transmitted to the attacker when his technique lands on the opponent.

REI (JP) The Japanese command to bow.

REVERSE KNIFE HAND A strike which uses the thumb edge of the hand. See also 'Ridge Hand'.

REVERSE PUNCH A strong punch, utilising the hips and characterised by having the opposite leg forward to the fist used, i.e., left punch/right forward foot.

REVERSE ROUNDHOUSE KICK A kick in which the heel, or sole of foot impacts on the target via a circular path.

RIDGE HAND See 'Reverse Knife Hand'.

RISING BLOCK A deflection block which protects the head.

ROLL OUT A technique used in Aikido, Hapkido and Shorinji Kempo, where a person being thrown literally rolls off their shoulder.

ROUNDHOUSE KICK See also 'Turning Kick'. A kick which uses the ball of the foot, or the instep. It is delivered in a circular path.

RYU (JP) A school, or method of practice of a martial art.

SAI (JP) A three pronged stabbing and clubbing weapon used by traditional Okinawan Karate schools.

SALUTATION The formal greeting in the training hall.

SAMURAI (JP) Literally 'One Who Serves'. One of the castes of Japanese warrior which later became to mean all true Japanese warriors.

SANCHIN (JP) A Karate kata derived from the Naha-te school of Okinawan Karate.

SANKUKAI (JP) A school of Japanese Karate.

SASH A coloured band worn around the body and used to denote rank.

SAVATE (FR) A French system of boxing and kicking related to but distinct from Thai Boxing.

SEIPAI (JP) A Karate kata based upon the Naha-te school of Okinawan Karate.

SEISHAN (JP) A Karate kata found in all three of the Okinawan Karate Schools.

SEIZA (JP) The formal kneeling position found in the Japanese arts.

SEMI CONTACT The name given to a form of sparring where blows may be landed with controlled force. It sometimes means a form of otherwise Full Contact sparring which excludes specified targets, such as the face and head.

SEMPAI (JP) The senior student grade below the instructor in a Japanese training hall.

SENSEI (JP) The instructor, or teacher.

SHAOLIN (CHI) The Temple in China where the hard forms of Chinese martial art were refined.

SHINAI (JP) The bamboo practice sword used in Kendo.

SHITO RYI (JP) A school of Karate founded by Kenwa Mabuni.

SHOBUIPPON (JP) A one point contest.

SHORINJI KEMPO (JP) See 'Nippon Shorinji Kempo'. Any form of Japanese art which claims to be a form of Shaolin Chinese Boxing.

SHOTOKAN (JP) A school of Japanese Karatedo founded by Gichin Funakoshi.

SHUKOKAI (JP) A school of Japanese Karate based upon Shito Ryu. See also 'Taniha Shitoryu'.

SHURIKEN (JP) Throwing stars, used as anti-personnel weapons.

SHURI-TE (JP) One of three original styles of Okinawan Karate.

SICKLE An agricultural implement used as a weapon by Okinawan Karateka.

SIDE KICK A kick using the heel/edge of foot, delivered out to the side of the body.

SILAT (ML) A Malaysian art using trips, throws and strikes.

SNAP A whiplash like action, used to develop power.

SNAP KICK A fast kick which relies upon a whiplash like delivery.

SOFT STYLE A style of Chinese martial art using internal power. See also 'Internal Style'.

SOLE OF FOOT The striking surface of the foot used in crescent kick.

SOO BAHK (KO) An ancient Korean martial art.

SOUTHERN STYLES The Shaolin systems of hard Chinese martial art practised in Southern China. Rigid stances and hand techniques characterise their practice.

SPARRING A form of practice where opponents engage each other in combat. The sparring may be arranged in advance, or it can be completely unprogrammed, as in Free Sparring.

SPEAR HAND A jabbing technique which utilises the finger tips.

SPORT KARATE A form of competition Karate where matches are fought and won on the basis of combat rules.

STABILITY Firm balance during the execution of a technique or in a particular stance.

STAFF A wooden pole of approximately two metres in length.

STAMPING KICK A kick which is directed downwards – such as at the instep, or knee.

STANCE The attitude, both physical and mental, taken by a martial artist.

STICKY HANDS A practice found in Chinese martial arts, where both opponents try to keep their hands and arms in constant contact with each other.

STRADDLE STANCE A stance in which the legs are spread and the knees rotated outwards over the feet.

STRIKING TECHNIQUES Techniques which impact upon a target.

STYLE A variety of martial art.

SUMO (JP) Japanese wrestling.

SWEEP A technique which catches the opponent's foot, or feet and unbalances him.

SYSTEM See 'Style'.

TACTICS The plan of techniques to be used to secure victory.

TAEKWONDO (KO) 'Hand/Foot Way', a Korean martial art word originated in 1955 by General Choi Hong Hi. It covered all the various native martial arts forms and represented a line of development from them, with the majority of input coming from Japanese systems.

TAI CHI CHUAN (CHI) 'Great Ultimate Fist', a form of internal Chinese martial art.

TAMESHIWARI (JP) The breaking techniques of Karate, where wood, bricks and tiles are used to test the force of a strike.

TA MO (CHI) Bodhidharma, the Indian monk who introduced Zen Buddhism to China.

TANG SHOU DAO (CHI) An alternative name for Chinese Boxing.

TANG SOO DO (KO) 'The Way of Tang Hand', a Korean system very similar to Shotokan Karatedo.

TANIHA-SHITORYU (JP) The correct name of Shukokai Karate style named after the originator, Chojiro Tani.

TAO (CHI) A Chinese term describing the presence of an energy or force which motivates all things.

TE (JP) 'Hand', as used to describe the Okinawan systems. See also 'Okinawa-te'.

THAI BOXING See Muay Thai. Thai Boxers use boxing gloves and fight in a boxing ring. Full power punches and kicks to the head are allowed.

TOMARI-TE (JP) One of the three original forms of Okinawan Karate.

TONFA (JP) The rice grinder handles used as covert weapons by Okinawan Karateka.

TUNIC Outfit worn to practice. See also 'Uniform'.

TURNING KICK See Roundhouse Kick.

UECHI-RYU (JP) A school of Okinawan Karate founded by Kanbun Uechi.

UNIFORM A training tunic. See also 'Tunic'.

UPPERCUT A close range punch that travels upwards into the target.

UPWARD BLOCK See 'Rising Block'.

VITAL POINTS See 'Pressure Point'. Areas of the body which when struck can prove fatal.

WADO RYU (JP) The 'Way of Peace' school of Japanese Karatedo founded by Hironori Ohtsuka.

WANSHU (JP) A Karate kata derived from the Tomari-te school of Okinawan Karate.

WAZA-ARI (JP) A scoring technique worth half an Ippon.

WEAPON Any part of the body, or extension thereof, which is used in combat.

WING CHUN (CHI) 'Beautiful Springtime', the name given to a style of hard Chinese Boxing by its founder, the Bhuddist nun, Ng Mui.

WRISTLOCK A hold applied to the wrist to immobilise it, or to be used as a lever in a throw.

WU SHU (CHI) 'Martial Arts', as in 'Bujitsu' (Jp). The military arts of China.

X BLOCK A form of block where both arms are used together and are crossed, the one over the other.

YAMEI (JP) The Japanese command to stop.

YANG (CHI) One half of the Chinese Taoist view of the universe. It is characterised by positive action.

YIN (CHI) The opposite of 'Yang', being negative in action.

ZEN (JP) A religious philosophy originating in India. See also 'Chan'.

Unlike Japan and Europe, the martial arts in the USA are almost totally decentralized (some would say chaotic). With few exceptions, such as judo, which has been an Olympic sport for men since 1964, and kendo, which is very small in terms of the number of practitioners, national organizations either do not exist or represent very small sub-groups.

Finding a sensei or sifu or sabumnim is rather like finding a doctor. You can get a name out of the local phone book or ask a local medical association for a reference from its list of licensed practitioners. No matter how you get the name, you must visit the doctor to find out if she or he is suitable. The martial arts work the same way. Once you have written to an organization to get the name of the representative of their specific style in your area, you still have to visit the school to check it out for yourself. A little common sense and creative shopping on the part of the potential student are at least as useful as a name culled from a membership list by someone who has never actually seen the member in question.

Once you have your list, whether from a national organization or from the phone book, spend some time observing classes. In a large school watch the head instructor at work as this person's attitudes will carry over to the junior instructors who will teach you as a beginner. Watch the beginners' classes to see what you will be getting into. Is this something you want to do? After watching two or three times do you still want to do it?

Do not mistake a martial arts school for a health club. There are good schools with no showers located in crumbling ghetto lofts; other fine schools are downright posh with weights, saunas, and juice bars. Good instructors also come in all shapes, sizes, and personalities. They can be male, female, black, white, and every shade of grey; young, old, very old; old-fashioned, up-to-date, outrageous; Buddhist monks, born-again Christians, atheists, nuns; Ph.Ds, high-school dropouts, look-alikes for Chuck Norris, the Dragon Lady, the Junkyard Dog, or Miss Marple. In other words, people. Like you.

If an instructor wearing a red, white and blue stars-and-stripes gi can be as competent as one wearing perfectly plain Japanese traditional whites, what can a beginner look for in evaluating these different schools? First, you cannot evaluate the instructor as a martial artist when you are a beginner. Rely on your instincts to evaluate the instructor as a person and the school as a place where you may be spending a great deal of time.

Is the school clean? The poorest students can keep the dojo clean and the richest can show respect the same way. A dirty dojo has gone too far from the Way. In 1970 it was still possible for a good school to have no women students.

Today you should wonder why there are no women or no women of senior rank. Ask. Do not be overly impressed by numbers. Different systems promote at different rates; some people simply do not go for promotion examinations and keep their same rank for 10 or 15 years; others outright fake it. Do not sign up for a contract longer than a few months at the beginning; if you are being pressured to commit yourself to a year's contract, leave. Of course, if you are not permitted to watch classes do not under any circumstances sign up.

If after watching a few classes you still want to try it, that is the best possible indication that you should do so.

The following is a partial list of persons and organizations that may be able to help you with information, especially with locating an instructor in your area. The inclusion or non-inclusion of any person or organization does not imply endorsement or non-endorsement of that person or organization.

AIKIDO
U.S. Aikido Federation
142 West 18th St.
New York NY 10011

Aikido Schools of Ueshiba
421 Butternut St., NW
Washington DC 20012

IAIDO
Japanese Swordsmanship Society
P.O. Box 1116
Rockefeller Ctr. Sta.
New York NY 10185

(see also Kendo Federation of the USA)

JAPANESE CLASSICAL WEAPONRY
(see Japanese Swordsmanship Society)

JUDO
U.S. Judo Inc.
Frank P. Fullerton
P.O. Box 637
El Paso TX 79944

U.S. Judo Ass'n
19 N. Union Blvd.
Colorado Springs CO 80909

U.S. Judo Federation
Yosh Yoshida
2530 Taravel St.
San Francisco CA 94116

KARATE
Seido Karate Organization
61 W. 23rd St.
New York NY 10010

Shorinji Kempo
Mr. Y. Miyata
301 W. 53rd St.
New York NY 10019

Japan Karate Federation
1930 Wilshire Blvd, #1208
Los Angeles CA 90057

U.S. Karate Ass'n
4309 N. 7th Ave.
Phoenix AZ 85013

AAU Karate
Mr. George Anderson
1300 Kenmore Blvd.
Akron OH 44320

KENDO
Kendo Federation of the USA
Mr. Gene Eto
1715 W. 256th St.
Lomita CA 90717

NAGINATA
Ms. Helen Nakano
The US Naginata Federation
22710 Elm Ave.
Torrance CA 90277

(on East coast see also Japanese Swordsmanship
Society)

TAEKWONDO
U.S. Taekwondo Union
Mr. Moo-Yong Lee
669-A Burnside Ave.
E. Hartford CT 06108

WOMEN
Fighting Woman News Quarterly
Box 1459, Grand Central Stn.
New York NY 10163

Girls' and Women's Taekwondo Newsletter and
U.S. Taekwondo Women's Committee
14125 Berryville Rd.
Germantown MD 20815

Nat'l Women's Martial Arts Federation
Ms. Bobbi Synder
1724 Sillview Dr.
Pittsburgh PA 15243